The Art
Of
Facing Your Fears

The Art

Of

Facing Your Fears

A LIFE COACHING GUIDE

Adriana Cara

To order additional copies of this book, contact:
Xlibris
844-714-8691
www.Xlibris.com
Orders@Xlibris.com
843751

TO ALL MY FEARFUL AND FEARLESS FRIENDS,

YOURS,
ADRIANA CARA

Contents

Note From The Author

FEARLESS IS NOT THE ABSENCE OF FEAR; IT
IS THE MASTERY OF FEAR.

ARIANNA HUFFINGTON

The idea of writing a book about FEAR started to grow in my mind way before my first project, the writing of my first book, **THE ART OF LOVE CONNECTION AND MARRIAGE** which was released in June of 2021 and took me several years in the making.

THE FEAR was my constant companionship since my first childhood memories...painful, debilitating, draining, humiliating and suffocating.

It was supposed to grow with me to dominate my soul and shape me into a shy and fearful person until I realized that I could conquer it.

Living in a family with limited beliefs, poor education and no exposure to the world and also being the second child put me in a place where I was never good enough...

Therefore, I had to fight hard to earn my love respect and consideration from my family.

Lacking the warmth of a nest and no reassuring feeling of belonging turned me into a difficult and fearful child.

I carried this burden into adulthood until life prepared a different path for me and I learned how to tame my fears, listen to my body and mind and act with courage.

Did I ever suppress all my fears?

Not always…

However, I found a way to live and deal with them and avoid falling into the abyss of impossibilities.

Fear is part of life, like love, hate, anger, greed.

It will always linger around like a silent enemy ready to attack.

However, we have to learn how to defend ourselves by any means.

Thanks to a life dedicated to coaching people and avidly reading books about self-improvement that shaped my life, I now understand the mechanism of fear.

I wrote this book with a lot of love and understanding for all the fearful and fearless people with my greatest hope that I will guide you into becoming a powerful individual with a serene life and peace of mind.

ADRIANA CARA

Definition Of Fear

ONCE YOU BECOME FEARLESS, LIFE BECOMES
LIMITLESS.

AMY MESA

FEAR is a powerful emotion caused by the feeling of close danger or a dangerous person that can cause pain, a threat or even death.

The word FEAR comes from the old English Word "FAER" meaning sudden calamity or danger and refers to justified fright.

It is the anxiety and uneasiness that can be physical (fight or flight reaction) or psychological.

Is the reaction of a real or imagined event?

Traditionally most people consider fear as a negative emotion therefore try "to push it under the rug" but in the reality FEAR has a very important role in keeping us safe and alert against a potential danger.

The physical immediate response is very strong and the stress hormone (cortisol and adrenaline) are released.

The heart rate is increasing, the body flow changes, the sweating is uncontrollable, the breathing becomes shallow and the skin tightens.

Still the spiritual meaning of fear is normal as a way to fulfill our destiny or to respond to God's demands.

The conclusion is to feel the fear, be aware, contemplate it and then let it go...

FEAR is the strongest and oldest emotion in humankind and in animal kingdom.

We all start with the fear of unknown as a basic trait.

Unfortunately, a fear reaction out of control can affect our decisions making in a negative way, leaving us susceptible to impulsive reaction.

Today we rely on medication, we are the Prozac generation and many of us are suffering from incurable fears, heart disease, inherited trauma, PTSD, Irritable Bowel Syndrome and many other conditions.

An "unknown source" created very interesting acronyms:

F.E.A.R

False
Evidence
Appearing
Real

False evidence of appearing real

Or

Future
Evidence
Appearing
Real

Future events appearing real.

We live in a world of disastrous pandemic; Covid 19 and lately the Monkey pox and all the variants created an additional fear that altered the life and the well-being of the humans.

We are afraid to go out to meet people and have a healthy social life; we cannot travel, enjoy life and help each other.

There is a paralyzing state of fear, we are afraid of getting sick, suffer, infect the loved ones or die.

Can we overcome FEAR or should we let it rule and destroy us?

I consider FEAR a way of resisting change and I am here with you to unfold the mystery of it, to find out about the anatomy of it and to discover a way to come to good terms with this deep emotion.

The Origins Of Fear

FEAR DOES NOT EXIST ANYWHERE EXCEPT IN
YOUR MIND.

DALE CARNEGIE

FEAR existed from the beginning of times, when LIFE appeared on
EARTH as part of EXISTENCE.

First, the single cell called amoeba, considered the first form of life,
struggled with fear to protect itself.

It did not have legs, brain or spinal cord but had the instinct of
survival.

Somewhere about 500 million years ago a part of our future brain
located in the fish brain on the evolution scale started to evolve.

It is a small organ located at the very base of the cortex called
amygdala.

Seth Godin called it "the lizard brain and it is by far the most
powerful part of the brain and without it, and we cannot exist and
survive.

The lizard brain sends emotional messages to the cortex and keeps us alert for any danger but does not know how to differentiate a big threat from a small one.

The moment life was created, so was fear, as a state of being, from birth to death.

All creature experience fear, all get scared and experience this powerful, unstable, unfamiliar, debilitating emotion that sometimes saves our life protecting us.

Fear is here to stay and we had better start to understand it because if you do not, you are in a serious state of denial.

Fear is when your mind is not taking instructions from you anymore.

Considering that, the human being has two significant faculties (memory and imagination) fear means that the imagination is out of control and you should reestablish a possible relationship with it instead of fighting it.

During history times, feeling emotions was considered frivolous and unnecessary and we tried to suppress it, push it down, repress.

Fear was not an option and we never thought that we could make peace with it or other emotions.

Now it is time to reconsider.

Fear And Folk Practices

TO ESCAPE FEAR YOU HAVE TO GO THROUGH IT NOT AROUND IT.

RICHIE NORTHON

People from different cultures embrace the FEAR and the attitude against it in different ways.

Some use plants with hallucinogenic effect, like marijuana or ayahuasca, practice very common in South America among shamans.

In Africa, people ingest clay to chase the fear away (geophagya).

In South Asia the healers practice COINING (rubbing the skin with the edge of a coin until it creates skin lesions) CUPPING (placing heating glass cups on the skin and creating a negative pressure) or MEXABUSTION (touching the skin with burning incense).

In New Guinea, people suffer from a certain "cargo anxiety" believing that an ancestral spirit will bring a valuable cargo full of better food while the delusional ones destroy the present stock of food.

In India, because of so much social pressure, women are afraid to go out without the male company of their sons, husbands or fathers; this sensitive pattern is also associated with the fear of taking a decision (decidophobia).

Part of religion is the belief in the existence of a supreme evil spirit, SATAN, the antagonist of GOD.

Christians believe that Satan was an angel who led a heavenly revolt because of his pride and jealousy and eventually was expelled from heaven and thrown in the underworld of HELL.

The medieval church developed a grotesque image of the devil with horns and tail, with supernatural powers to tempt the sinners.

Moreover, the WITCHES appeared...sold their souls to Lucifer and were punished to death by burning their bodies.

Studies show that the EXORCISM and ANTI WITCH were still present in the third world in the sixties accompanied by demonological and astrological remedies.

Later the Christians produced art and literature with elaborate descriptions of Hell fact that increased the fear but did not solve the dilemma of explaining the presence of Evil in a world ruled by God.

The philosopher Plato described the fear of punishing after death even in the 4th century BC.

Another aspect is the presence of GHOSTS or spirits of the dead; they are the victims of murder, criminals or witches and are easily angered.

In the Indian culture where life extends beyond the body, ghost are considered a combination of time memory and energy.

When the memory is still active, the ghosts feel like humans.

Most of the times it happens when the dead person suffered a car accident, murder or suicide and the presence is still dense for a long time.

Ghosts are not dangerous because they do not have a conscious intention.

They do not have an intellect and they act by tendency.

It has also said that the ghosts have an unfinished karma.

They follow the living persons until there are some rituals done to put the ghosts to peace.

MAGIC is also a concern and it is connected with a desire of touching a greater power to defeat the fear.

Magicians consider themselves being a replica of God and try to expand their power accordingly, not by the progress of the science but by holding on to mysterious secrets.

They affirm that their power is divine therefore it cannot be taught but must be feared.

As we see historically, many fears are attributed to superstitions, witchcraft, demonology and evil spirit.

Experts believe that many basic fears are hardwired into the human brain as an automatic internal protection system.

The primordial fears existed before prerecorded history and they adapted in time.

Of course, during existence of the humans fears evolved and modified.

For example, the cave man was afraid of predators while the modern man could be afraid of driving...myself included.

Fears have something in common: they attack our senses of hearing, seeing, tasting, touching, smelling, and more and more fears appear in the modern world with new classification and nomenclature.

Today millions of people are trapped in fears and phobias but we are lucky that we live in a time of multiple possibilities.

We have access to literature, treatments, self-improvements methods and multiple therapies to ease the anguish of fear around the globe.

Fear Up Close And Personal

HAVE THE FEARLESS ATTITUDE OF A HERO
AND THE LOVING HEART OF A CHILD.

SOYEN SHAKU

I consider myself a very fortunate human being.

Life showed me so many faces of FEAR and as a result I became a better person, more humble, more compassionate and understanding, and above all more appreciative.

I will take this opportunity to share with you some memories that hunted me forever and will stay with me as part of my life.

I was born in a communist country where FEAR was a way of life.

My father was a prominent communist figure and I grew up in this spirit. I did not even have the chance to be baptized in a church but at home in hiding.

The Bible was forbidden and the churches were torn down or closed.

Growing up and being more aware of the political disaster and the imminent poverty following in my country I started to feel the rope of fear and frustration tightening more and more around my neck and the glimmer of hope through running away took shape.

We were all afraid to talk openly or make friends with the so called instigators and complain about the misery and the poverty around us.

I remember the bitter cold in the house because we did not have any heat in the winter, the famine and the hunger when we lived on food stamps and trying to buy bread or milk after long hours and fights on line, mostly in the night like in the war time.

The abortion was forbidden and the poor kids born by mistake were sent to orphanages and their fate was sealed.

As a child, I was always curious and avid of knowing but unfortunately, all the doors to culture were closed; books were forbidden except the one praising the communism, the TV had just a channel from 8 pm to 10 pm brainwashing people about the benefits of the communism.

I learned about ART thanks to my father's stamps collection...I fell in love with Dali, Picasso Van Gogh...

I was thinking more and more of fleeing...but if caught I could face death or labor camp.

However, what kind of life is this...in fear and ignorance?

I crossed the border in paralyzing fear with just water in my bag but unfortunately, I was caught close to the border and incarcerated, feeling defeated and broken.

While waiting for the sentence to be sent to a camp labor in a salt mine the impossible happened: the Revolution changed the whole status and I became a hero overnight.

I bought a one-way ticket to FREEDOM, the refugee camp in Austria.

There I faced different fears. Fear of being murdered or raped by other refugees, fear of not getting food for the day, fear that I will be sent back to my country.

After months of evaluations and interrogations I started slowly and timidly a new life.

I remember the first time when I went to a regular food store. So much blinding light, so warm, so much food, even watermelon in the winter...I was in a state of shock...never to forget.

It took me a lot of courage not to look back and to adapt to an uprooted life in a foreign country with new rules, new life, and new language and above all to a new way of fighting the attitude of the locals towards refugees.

I was swallowing my tears and frustration that I was born in the wrong country and I had to fight hard for everything but finally came to the country of my dreams, America, and started a life full of accomplishments.

I traveled the world and I was happy for the rich and cried for the poor.

I learned to value myself, to get rid of the past nightmares and see the light at the end of the tunnel.

I have friends and enemies, some love me some hate me, some give me things some steal from me...

I fell and got up, hoped and came to the brink of despair, but I am still a happy child in my heart.

There will be always someone to judge me for my birth country or for my accent but I look at the bigger picture and I am proud of who I became.

Just the fact that you are reading my humble thoughts on a piece of paper is the most valuable accomplishment of my life.

THANK YOU!

Political Fear

FEAR is as old as life and deep embedded in any living organism; it survived extinction through evolution.

It is created by danger, intimidation, war, politics and religion.

The human tendency of fear is a real feast for the politicians who exploit it for personal interests.

When the demagogues manage to get hold of our fear the humans often regress to an emotional strong state, illogical, tribal, aggressive, and is successfully used for their own agenda.

"The use of disinformation to promote fear is quite striking when we look at how in recent years some political matters have been increasingly spreading conspiracy theories" says Karen Douglas PhD at the University of Kent.

To win the supporters, the politicians use media to separate one another on different reasons, but if we spend more time together, we realize that we are all the same, weak or strong, funny or dumb, fearful or fearless.

Looking at planet Earth from space, we don't see any defined borders, skin color, religion hate or fear.

When the president Franklin Delano Roosevelt was elected on March 4th 1933 the country hit the bottom of Great Depression.

The semi-paralyzed president addressed the nation:

"So, first of all let me assert my firm belief that the only thing that we have to fear is FEAR itself, nameless, unreasoning, unjustified terror which paralyzes needed efforts to convert retreat into advance."

The Great Depression could hurt the United States but fear could destroy it.

RISK and FEAR are main topics among sociologists and we live in a culture of fear: fear of terrorism, stalkers, internet, drugs, pedophiles, climate change, satanic cults, school shooting, cataclysms, cancer, Covid and war.

We are increasingly afraid and more at risk than ever.

BUT...we also know that we are fortunate that we live in a Western civilized country and we are the most prosperous humans in the history of the species.

If we put some numbers together, we are the healthiest, wealthiest, longest-lived people in the history.

The greatest paradox is that we are afraid...and the internet and the big companies are the merchants of fear.

Moreover, this is why there are so few possibilities to make money by promoting the fact that we are healthy and safe.

The powerful people on top of the pyramid make high profits by creating fear.

After September 11 2001, people are terrified by terrorism.

George W. Bush spoke these words on September 12 when smoke still rose from the rubble at World Trade Center:

"Freedom and democracy are under attack."

Besides fear, we felt sorrow, grief hate and rage.

Terrorism became a universal obsession and the high end Security Business became overnight the business of the future.

Only the Land Security companies went from 15 to 861 in 3 years after the attack.

In the meantime The Health Care System remained so precarious that in a long run the lack of it was more costly that the money spent on counter terrorism.

Covid-19 with all the variants scared the whole planet and disrupted the basic existence of the global population and completely destroyed the social life of the individuals.

However, companies like Pfizer or Johnson & Johnson are booming trying to create vaccines...and yet not cure.

Still the miracle of life is unfolding better than ever, we live longer and healthier.

Still fear is there...the hideous predator ready to bite.

Is our purpose in life to fall victim of fear or are we ready to fight and rise?

What are you afraid of?

Why are you so afraid?

Why do we put ourselves in false danger and fear things that are not real?

THE SCIENCE OF FEAR holds the answer.

Covid-19 The Big Fear

NOTHING IN LIFE IS TO BE FEARED, IT IS ONLY
TO UNDERSTAND.
NOW IS THE TIME TO UNDERSTAND MORE SO
THAT WE FEAR LESS.

MARIE CURIE

I write this chapter right after THE POLITICAL FEAR because I consider that there is a great connection between the two of them.

The outbreak of covid-19 (Corona Virus Disease) in 2019 turned into a global crisis taking the population by storm psychologically, by inflicting severe feelings of fear, insecurity and anxiety.

The misleading and the misconception introduced by mass media and the governmental policies became stronger by the day.

The speculations and contradictory data expressed by experts, researchers and scientific societies transformed the mental global condition into a phobic disaster.

As a result, all of us experience psychological disorders with the appearance of damages of mental health, with worsening symptoms of fear, anxiety, phobias and depressions.

People disinfect mail and food, rub themselves with alcohol, refuse to get out of the house, think twice before returning to work or refuse to socialize.

The testing for covid-19 became an obsession. People with or without symptoms spend time in line for testing with the risk of catching the virus there.

The more we listen to the media the more fearful we become ignoring the fact that we have to protect ourselves not only from the virus but also from the FEAR itself simultaneously.

Americans believe that 50% of the people who die of covid-19 are 55 and older but it is actually 92%, so the virus mostly attacks old people with preexisting conditions or low immunity.

When we hear about children hospitalized in intense care units we become frightened.

We should start flatten the fear with facts; the recent statistics show that children under 18 are 2% of the total number of children (74 millions) in US.

Children die from many other diseases or preexisting conditions and the big picture concludes that the death due to covid-19 among children is very low.

There are so many theories about how the virus was born: a wild animal for dinner, a mistake in the chemical lab, a political manipulation or the start of a biological war for supremacy.

Every theory has an explanation, has pro and con that makes the people more fearful, confused and divided.

The truth is that a pandemic of this proportion was expected but unfortunately, no one took action to prevent it or even stop it at the first sign.

The panic exploded. The heads of the states were caught by surprised and shut down the borders installing severe restrictions and before all...FEAR.

"It will go away...," said president Trump about the virus a long time ago.

This particular virus ended up by being one of the most different, strong and contagious than any other experienced along the history.

Being so easy transmissible, it attacks the respiratory track and many people ended up in hospital on ventilators and survived with severe health complications or died.

The body absorbs the virus and the message of sickness or death is sent to the brain creating a maddening state of fear.

The big problem is that covid-19 spreads among asymptomatic people and is constantly mutating fact that makes the virus a silent killer.

It is impossible to predict or to keep up with the accuracy and efficiency of the latest antivirus Vaccine.

Only the thought that people have to be isolated when infected or suspect of carrying the virus is terrifying.

People die and the loved ones mourn them on zoom, children are born in isolation, schools are open and closed.

We are even more confused because the rules and restrictions of the pandemic are different from state to state, governor to governor, president to president.

In addition to being an illness that is now incurable, COVID-19 also causes political unrest and widespread terror.

New variants are born with a maddening speed, so we fall back when comes to a cure.

The government is controlling the population breaking the rules of HIPPA and the patients confidentiality by tracking the people's communication devices.

Still covid is a mystery...a virus or a political weapon.

We are forced to have the vaccine and booster after booster with no real result.

Small children are vaccinated.

People get ill every day and China was in lock down again, with very strong repercussion for the global economy.

The debate about wearing the mask is maddening the people.

Is it ever going to get better or is it going to be a way of life?

WE ARE DYING OF FEAR.

The name for this condition is THANATOPHOBIA or death anxiety with severe mental repercussions.

However, there is hope, and until the situation will be more or less acceptable, we need to practice some self-discipline exercises to quiet our mind and face this horrible fear more easy.

LET US TRY SOME TECHNIQUES:

1. Breathing deeply, the brain sends automatically a signal when to breathe but this time we talk to the brain and focus on long deep breath...10, 20 seconds if possible.
2. Try to change your behavior when watching the news going from compulsory to sporadically; there will still be a lot of uncertainty about the virus and the inducing fear and trauma of uncertainty is an additional stress.
3. Focus on things that give you peace of mind: adopt an animal, find a hobby, call friends and family(no texting) more often, put the mask and go for a walk, cook the favorite food, help the community create a support group on line.
4. Show gratitude and connect with people; remember how people showed their respect for the medical staff by making noise every day at 7pm.
5. Why so depressed?

Look in the mirror and smile!

We still have a roof over the head, food on the table, electricity, the government helped any possible way by stimulus checks of free food, we have hot water, we have books and Netflix, and we can still enjoy our favorite song.

Have you even for a second thought about the poor people living in deep poverty, famine, and lack of medical health?

Or the communist countries where the war poverty and oppression is the way of life?

And still here people get suicidal because they don't know what to do with their time...

6. GET VACCINATED!!!!

This is the way of ending this pandemic at least so far...

I know...you might say that the vaccine became a political issue but us, the regular people do not have the time and the resources to contradict the benefits of the vaccine; but we clearly see that the vaccinated people have more chances to get mild symptoms if getting the virus.

Moreover, we do not have another smarter and immediate alternative.

Even if we doubt the efficacy of the vaccine, I consider that being vaccinated is an act of love for your neighbor and compassion for others and an act of showing respect for the ones who died of covid-19.

We also know from the history of the pandemic that the vaccine is the most efficient cure.

It breaks my heart when I see people in US mock and refuse the vaccination while some other ones in poor countries do not have access to it.

C.E.P.I. (The Coalition for Epidemic Preparedness Innovations) is form as a liaison between governments and funding companies in order to develop the right vaccine and make it available for everybody from everywhere otherwise we cannot heal the world of this deadly plague.

Unfortunately, the political question will be "Who can afford to get vaccinated?"

Is the race for vaccine going to unite the HUMANITY and raise enough money to end this pandemic?

Time will tell...we are still in the middle of it and not getting any better...

I am revising this chapter almost 4 months after I wrote it...nothing changed, we are still in the same dark hole of the pandemic.

In the meantime, a new long lock down in China that is brutally crippling the economy, which is in a great state of collapse.

People are dying, new variants of covid are breaking out and we cannot keep up with the speed of the pandemic.

In addition, out of the blue...the monkey pox.

Some other viruses are being born, a hepatitis in young children that require transplant and it is not (or is it???) related to covid is breaking out in the world.

So far, Covid pandemic is a way of life and we have to adapt no matter the consequences.

The government is putting the blame on the pandemic and the war in Ukraine for the inflation, which is affecting the day-to-day life leading go poverty.

Is the end near?

Fear And Putin's War

IF WARS CAN BE STARTED BY LIES, THEY CAN
BE STOPPED BY TRUTH.

JULIAN ASSANGE

I write this chapter while my heart is crying tears of blood, hoping that until you, my friend and precious reader will enjoy my book and there will be peace in the World.

We witness one of the most atrocious carnage in the History of the Humanity, an attack against civilians, children, and mothers, old and young.

Regular people join the soldiers to defend their country and their values.

People die...others flee to save their lives living everything behind.

Others are kidnapped and dragged to Russia like cattle.

Putin faces the biggest disappointment of his life: Ukrainians are building a shield with their bodies and refuse to surrender.

We all hope that the Russian soldiers will turn their weapons against their own dictator.

But until then it will be more distress, blood and suffering and a beautiful country is turning into rubble under our own eyes...

There was never such a strong response for help from NATO, but still we kneel in front of a despot that has the whole world wrapped around his finger and in a tantrum, he can destroy the Humanity including himself with just a press of the button on a nuclear weapon.

The World is holding its breath...

This war is actually an ongoing war between Russia and Ukraine since 2014 when the Russians invaded Crimea, originally a Ukrainian territory.

Ukraine was part of the Soviet Empire until 24th of August 1991 when it became an independent state.

History tells of a proud nation that has inhabited its territory with its Slavic culture since 32,000 BC and is considered a key to the European economy.

The evolution of this proud nation was against the dark desires of Putin, who always thought or rebuilding the Russian Empire and subduing with force any state that would not surrender through terror and intimidation.

But his ego and his person is pushed against the wall...hopefully crushed soon.

In a world decimated by the pandemic, ruled by fears and politics there are still people supporting this war?

This is how it is...the Humanity is more fearful, vulnerable and submissive to the horrors of the war.

The neighboring countries part of NATO are overwhelmed by the wave of Ukrainian refugees but they are helping as much as they can even that they fear of becoming a target for the Russian army.

We all wait, short of breath, holding our tears, with a bitter taste about what is happening in the 21st century...

Maybe the history will talk about Putin's war, the global fear, and the genocide that he provoked ...

But for sure the history will talk about the heroism and resilience of the Ukrainian people and their patriotism, their pride in defending their country with any risk involved.

Until then... let's pray in a Universal voice for a Universal God and for a Universal love for the Humanity!

I visit this chapter like the one before this because I needed some update before I send my manuscript to the editor.

There are almost 3 months since this war started and the only thing that changed is that it is not Breaking news any more...it continues with a menace until the country and the people will be erased from the map.

Putin is not giving up and continues the massacre of the civilians and people who are left to fight in Ukraine (85% of the population fled to some neighboring countries or US).

Besides the human loss, which is beyond comprehension (mass human graves), the financial loss is absolutely huge and the states of NATO send help to patch up the damage that Russia does every day. US is expected to pay 250mil a day as a recovery plan to help Ukraine for at least 5 months...is it going to help?

There is talk about nuclear attack and Putin celebrates with nonchalance the victory over the Nazi in the WW2 in a public display of weapons to create more intimidation.

It seems that the end of the war is not very near...

The Human Needs

EVERYTHING YOU EVER WANTED IS SITTING
ON THE OTHER SIDE OF FEAR.

GEORGE ADDAIR

To understand the anatomy of FEAR and all the other negative emotions, we have to experience and validate our needs.

Failure to attend them will have painful repercussions in our life and will create a solid ground for the birth of FEAR.

The topic of the human needs was always a very controversial one because even if we are all human beings with the same anatomical and physiological structure we are different from one another through our priorities and emotional status.

I incorporated this chapter in my book to explain how important is to acknowledge and fulfill our basic needs so that we will not have too much room left to develop powerful and negative emotions like fear.

There are different theories about the human needs.

Sigmund Freud was the father of creating the HUMAN NEEDS PYRAMID with the first step made of the basic physiological needs (thirst, hunger, breathing sleeping, and sex).

Abraham Maslow, another psychologist created another hierarchy of human needs, a little different from Freud, and in tight relation with the human chakras (energy points):

1.   Physiological needs (the ones we mentioned before) related to the first chakra located at the base of the spine, called ROOT.
2.   Safety, security of the body, family and property; this is in alignment with the second chakra located below the navel and called SACRAL.
3.   Belonging, friendship, family, intimacy, all related to the third chakra, the HEART.
4.   Self-esteem, confidence, achievement, respect for one another.
5.   Self-actualization, morality, creativity, spontaneity.

The fourth and fifth human needs are related to the THROAT, THIRD EYE AND CROWN in the chakra system.

Maslow emphasizes the importance of BELONGING as a major human need.

We need to belong to ourselves before we belong to others.

We have more than seven billions versions of human needs unfolding every day; they motivate our personal decisions and actions.

Each of us has a special filter of perception and sometimes we are not quite aware or fully conscious of the decision-making or why we make it.

According to Tony Robbins, the well-known life coach, there are 6 human needs that influence our behavior, deepest motivation and decisions making.

Going from a pyramid to a linear system the human needs move from a personal and material level to a powerful interaction and energy in the world.

We cannot create a permanent personal chart of our needs because our life is in constant change; we grow and we have different priorities to fulfill during our life.

A modern accurate list of HUMAN NEEDS to this point in the evolution of humanity seems to be the following:

1. CERTAINTY

The need of comfort and satisfaction, the security that we pass our DNA to our children.

It means covering the basics, doing the needed work, paying the bills and secure a roof over the head.

The negative side of this need appears when we create a wall to stay in a comfort zone and resist the change.

The good side is the stability and trust in the continuous changing life.

The questions arising from this content are:

a.   What are the ways to achieve the feeling of certainty in our life?
b.   Are you satisfying the basic physiological needs?
c.   Do you do anything special to accomplish your needs?
d.   Do you have empowering beliefs or religious ones?
e.   Do you focus in the past or in the future?

2. UNCERTAINTY (VARIETY)

This is opposite to certainty and means the need of challenge, change, stimulation and evolution; it is also getting out of boredom, predictability and stagnation.

The risk of embracing uncertainty is the fear of unknown, the fear of failure.

The positive aspect is the continuous dynamical movement in our life, the need of change in relationships, jobs and decision taking.

The questions related to variety are:

a.   What do you do to bring variety in your life?
b.   Do you have fears, hesitations, personal problems that will bring the feeling of emotional or financial uncertainty in your life?
c.   What are you afraid of?

The first human needs in this chart work as polarities with each other and create a force that makes us a whole. Our life with missing one or another would be incomplete and out of balance.

3.   SIGNIFICANCE

This is the need to be wanted, validated, special, unique, and important for whom we are and what we do. It creates a sense of identity in the world and makes us feel independent and powerful.

The negative aspect of this human need is that it can make us addicted to different aspects of our life like career and we can lose touch with our loved ones.

It can also create the fear of "I am not good enough".

In the positive way, it is the power of acknowledgment, integrity, and expression for ourselves and the people around us.

Here are some questions to this subject:

a.   How do you become significant?
     Through violence or love?
b.   Does it affect your health, relationship or career?

4.   LOVE AND CONNECTION

This is a subject that I simply love, and I expressed myself in my book THE ART OF LOVE, CONNECTION AND MARRIAGE, released last year.

We all need love and intimacy, we need to be loved and feel that we belong.

We simply need the human touch. Period!

Some people choose love some others prefer just connections.

We need love permanently or temporarily, we also need to love our self and ultimately God.

The bad side is that people get afraid of a broken heart.

But...the wonderful feeling of falling in love is powerful and rewarding.

Here we also have questions:

a. How do you give or receive love?
b. Do you do specifically something and what is it?
c. Are you afraid and hold your love back in order not to become a victim?
d. Are you doing something to conquer the fear of falling in love?
e. Do you need to go out of your comfort zone in order to fall in love?

As we go on with the list we see that the four human needs that we just talked about so far are referred as "personality needs" because they are centered on the individual quest to self-fulfillment and personal achievements.

The next two human needs are more complex, and are defined as "the needs of the spirit", and represent a step further to achieving happiness and bliss in all aspects of life.

5. GROWTH

It is the need of physical, emotional, intellectual and spiritual growth.

The law of survival is GROWTH in all area of existence.

Our right is to expand and to break the barriers of limitations.

The negative point of this act is "the fear of not being ready" or "the fear of not being enough" and it will drive us to postpone actions for unlimited time.

The good of it is the acceptance and the acknowledgment that GROWTH is a journey not a destination; it allows us to be authentic, ready to learn and transform.

6. CONTRIBUTION

Is the need to serve and be beneficial to others as well as protect loved ones? This need is solidly supported by the needs we previously talked about and brings a purpose to life.

We can bring a contribution to our community by volunteering or just being at the service to the world, to the people and animals that need support.

This action has an immense power on our spiritual growth.

My humble contribution to the world is to share my knowledge through this book with you, dear reader, and hopefully bring a ray of light and joy in your existence.

The question is:
Is your contribution beneficial to anybody?

Due to personal development in our life, we value different needs in different times.

We need to have a positive balance between all of them, validate them and get the most of each of them.

The six human needs are generally classified, but if there were a seventh or more, what would that be and how would it be fulfilled?

Only YOU can answer...

But what happens to us if the alignment of our needs is broken?
Sigmund Freud created also a list of FIVE NATURAL TENDENCIES even though the concept was well known in the ancient Eastern Psychology; it can answer the question above.

The five Natural Tendencies are:

1. ANGER

Most of the people experiencing this tendency remain angry and difficult to satisfy looking constantly to find a way to disagree.

The narcissists and the alpha personalities fall in this category mostly going all the way to support their theory even if it is wrong.

The antidote and the wisdom coming out of anger is to accept things the way they are, to stop disagreeing and remain calm and satisfied with the outcome of the situation.

2. DENIAL

For the people of this group the change required is difficult and painful and they prefer to avoid or postpone a situation.

There is a constant NO in their reality and they mostly fantasize than act.

The antidote is to open your eyes and overcome any uncomfortable circumstances and become aware and conquer the weakness; it will lead to the right attitude and strategy.

3. DESIRE

The people ruled by desire want to make all the things at once.

They have difficulties reaching the goal or the solution and they create a state of suffering and hopelessness for themselves.

The good advice is to allow the solution to come to them without any effort, to surrender to the Laws of Universe and to find a natural rhythm between WANTING and ACHIEVING.

4. JEALOUSY

The people of this family compare themselves constantly with the ones around, secretly wanting to contribute to the misfortunes of the others.

The perfect German definition for this feeling is SCHADENFREUDE.

Schadenfreude comes from the German words schaden (harm) and freude (joy). It means pleasure or joy derived from someone else suffering or misfortune.

Anatomically, when we feel schadenfreude the portion of the brain devoted to feelings of empathy shuts down while the "feel good" area is getting more stimulated.

This feeling is born out of fear and powerlessness.

The only way to shift their perspective is to transform the jealousy into acceptance and become more giving and more generous.

5. PRIDE

These people secretly feel that they are smarter, cleverer and they consider having a better status.

Being a citizen of the world I experienced myself situations related to this tendency.

I was born in a communist country by misfortune and tried to make a decent living abroad. I was underestimated and considered a less valuable human being... but I overcame this malevolence.

The perfect way to overcome pride is to practice equality among people regardless of color, religion, and look, country of birth or sexual orientation.

6. GUILT (the concept is not on the list)

This feeling helps nobody, encourages negative behavior and perpetrates the cycle of making things worse than better.

People find comfort in food, drugs, alcohol and chain smoking.

The right attitude to conquer the guilt is to assess the situation first, make a list with your mistakes and create a positive and constructive way of thinking.

The empowering thought to conquer the guilt will be:
"Next time I will…" instead of "If only I had…"
Acceptance will turn the vicious cycle of guilt into a virtuous one.

The meaning and the goal of writing this chapter is to learn to accept our tendency that "feeling low" or "feeling down" is a normal part of life.

It can take us out of the cocoon of false security that we created around ourselves due to fear.

It will help us fight against negative behavior and learn to accept our feelings and ourselves.

We all feel desire, hate, love, fear and ultimately grow.

The power to overcome our obstacles is within us and ultimately we will we will FIND Peace and ALIGNMENT with all our NEEDS.

Ultimately, we will seek the divine connection with THE SUPREME POWER, which relates to the seventh chakra, THE CROWN.

Until then we have to do a lot of constructive thinking and acting.
Everything is possible with a lot of faith, love and above all WITH NO FEAR.

Fear...Friend Or Foe?

IF YOU DON'T KNOW THE NATURE OF FEAR,
THEN YOU CAN NEVER BE FEARLESS.

PEMA CHODRON

Do you know that the most important relationship in your life is the one with FEAR?

It is the relationship with yourself and if you want to have an authentic relationship with yourself, you had better bond with your fear because you and your fear have to coexist together.

We have to understand that FEAR is part of who we are and we cannot fix it but we can fix ourselves.

The first time when you say "I AM AFRAID" there will always be somebody to say "There is nothing to be afraid of" or "Think positive" in other words fear is not necessary and there is no need for you to suffer...

REALLY?

Controlling fear is like controlling breathing; you can do it for little but not for long.

You can walk around feeling fearless, but the moment you drop your guard, the fear comes back stronger than ever; it can't be denied for long. Many of us refuse to face our fears and end up in the "happy world" of drugs, alcohol and excessive food.

We do not like our fear... that means we do not like ourselves and the result is that the fear grows bigger.

The situation itself deteriorates and we end up single and vulnerable and life becomes more suppressed and dysfunctional.

Finally, you will start controlling everybody else because you cannot control yourself.

The stored feelings of fear will force the body to compensate and the result is a general state of malaise.

You will become numb, inflate like a balloon and burst.

It is like controlling a volcano.

The harder you work to control your fears the more you lose touch with yourself and others and you will end up emotionally crippled, phobic, obsessive and addictive.

Suppressing your fears is like a modern lobotomy, it is anesthetizing your brain.

The constant denial of fears brings a state of burnout, physically and emotionally, and will get tighter and tighter; the more you control the worse you feel.

Do you really think that suppressing your fear is going to help you achieve your goal or is it the denial of it that keeps you back from evolving?

Imagine how much easier our life would be if we can allow ourselves to say I FEEL AFRAID, I FEEL ABUSIVE OR ABUSED, AND I FEEL WRONG.

That would release a lot of tension that otherwise remains locked in the dark side of your brain.

LET US SHOW FEAR SOME RESPECT AND CONSIDERATION!

Why not honor it, feel it and give yourself the chance to be who you really are?

Try to stop controlling it; instead feel and experience all the emotions that show up.

Is it possible or is it too hard?

Let us look at FEAR like just fear, not an overwhelming state of mind or a battle you have to win.

When you are ready to feel your fear there will be a beginning, a peak and a decline and it will be more normal than we think.

Feeling emotions is healthy, it is part of human nature and we can express them in a personal way without repression; feel free to cry, scream, argue, and hit a wall...

Feel the feeling of fear with reverence and patience until it goes away; imagine a dark cloud of rain going by and spilling some water and eventually making room for the sun to shine.

Without FEAR, life will be boring, without heights and lows, without contrasts or progress...

Would you really like to be surrounded just by pink pillows and bliss?

Going the opposite way, admitting and facing your fears will calm you down and believe it or not will relax you.

Susan Jeffers said: "Pushing through fear is less frightening than living with underlying fear that comes from a feeling of helplessness."

The energizing variation of an uplifting mantra would be "I AM POWERFUL AND I LOVE IT!"

Let's have some food for the thoughts:

This power inside you lives you free and lets you do whatever you want, otherwise you will lose the sense of peace and you will be in a fearful place again.

A self-assured person attracts the power like a magnet.

Love and power go together and with no power, there is no love.

Life is a struggle and a learning experience, an adventure and an opportunity to take risks and from "I should" we can go to "I could".

It is worth taking the risk; it will give you a sense of valor and will enhance the ability to deal with fear.

Just figure out what you want to do, set your goals and work towards them.

Reclaim your power.

Avoid blaming yourself or the external forces.

Make your enemies your friends.

Don't wait for anybody to determine how to live your life.

Choose your path and follow it.

Create your own reality.

Move from a position of fear to a position of power.

Surround yourself with good energy and good people.

Look to improve yourself through self-improvement classes, seminars.

Chose the right path for your personal growth.

Let the people around you feel good and support them in a loving nurturing way.

Be your best friend and act with love around you.

Make healthy decisions and accept the new challenge in life.

Go with your guts and make the right decisions that fit you the best.

Focus on priorities.

Accept responsibilities.

Correct the mistakes.

Reach your goal.

Give yourself a leisure time, love and pamper yourself.

Relax and clear your mind.

Don't let the bitterness of the day interfere with these precious YOU moments.

Don't chase your fears, become present in the moment.

Experience the miracle of dealing with your deepest darkest fears and let them go.

Feel all your emotions and you will get something beautiful and beneficial at the end.

Remember that denial is deadly.

Acknowledge your pain and fear face them and say YES to them.

Be thankful for who you are and what you have and start giving away more love.

Take time to consciously and consistently focus on your spiritual path and experience joy, satisfaction and connection with the Supreme Force.

Learn how to bring light and powerful energy in your life.

The secret is making the negative forces work for you not against you.

You will experience what life has to offer, good or bad, you will notice, feel inspired and complete and you will grow.

Become a worrier and make FEAR your ally and you will feel a significant change in your life.

And YES, it will be a hard road to follow, full of darkness and bumps but it will bring the light shinier than before...i promise you.

The Anatomy Of Fear

IT IS NOT ABOUT BEING FEARLESS, IT'S ABOUT ACTING IN SPITE OF FEAR.

VERONICA ROTH

Before we start to study the **ANATOMY OF FEAR**, it is important to explore the **ANATOMY OF THE BRAIN** because this is the place where all begins...

THE ANATOMY OF THE BRAIN

1. AMYGDALA

Sometime 500 million years ago a part of our future brain, AMYGDALA first showed in fish evolved eventually into the human brain.

As I mention before Seth Godin called it **THE LIZARD BRAIN** and it is a small compound of the brain located at the base of the cortex, in shape of an almond.

It is by far the most powerful part of the brain, and without it we cannot survive.

THE LIZARD BRAIN sends emotional messages, being alert for anything that can kill us but does not really distinguish a small threat from a big one.

AMYGDALA labels emotions like ANGER and FEAR and determines how we feel about something way before the rational brain can assess the danger.

It does not use logic to come to conclusions and we feel the danger chills throughout our body.

AMYGDALA sends us in the mood of FIGHT (defending ourselves) or FLIGHT (running away or freeze).

It is very uncomfortable to undergo all those emotions especially if the threat is not evident but classified as dangerous.

2. PFC (PREFRONTAL CORTEX)

It is THE THINKING BRAIN, and it is your planner, organizer, decision maker and interpreter.

It sorts through incoming input (what you see, what you hear, smell, touch) and stores memories.

The PFC helps navigate through current situations and reviews the learned lessons in order to maximize a successful living.

There is a two ways relationship between your AMYGDALA and PFC and it helps to calm down in the moment of immediate threat by thinking more efficiently.

3. HIPPOCAMPUS

It is the storage and retrieval brain and creates long or short-term memories.

It also go through positive and negative highly emotional moments.

Think of your brain as a powerful highway with endless connections between billions of brain cells (neurons) or as a strong computer hardware.

The wiring helps us experience the world around us, feel the feelings we have and take actions to reach our goals.

This big complex organ helps us survive and thrive.

Humans have the advantage of thinking and outsmarting times of challenges while the animals who could not adapt go extinct.

We need to take risks, move forward and evolve.

THE FACES OF FEAR

FEAR arises as a normal response to a threat that can be real or imaginary.

It may cause uneasiness and unpleasant feelings including terror, the urge to escape, palpitations, trembling, nausea, sweating and the urge to cry or urinate.

As unpleasant as it is, fear is a normal and useful emotion, and it is considered an appropriate response to a concrete, real danger.

The great fear, called the "neurotic fear," should not be accepted by the conscious mind.

But there are still people who expose themselves to danger for the thrill produced by fear and ultimately enjoy it (racing cars, rope walking, bullfighting).

Fear is so complex and complicated; it can be fear of objects, people or fear of God.

Some scientists came with the idea of creating a "Fear inventory survey scale" in order to create more methods of therapies and counseling.

I will nominate some of the fear that most of the individuals experienced at least once in their lifetime.

1. FEAR OF THE UNKNOWN

There is the surprise of reality, life, death, God, the Universe, and what will happen in our lives next. This fear is one of the oldest fears and is helping us to go through everyday life from dangerous situations to facts.

If you feel intensely upset and anxious when you encounter an unknown situation you may develop a state of mind called "intolerance to uncertainty" meaning that the actual uncertain situation that you experience is intolerable leading to the impossibility to cope with the events.

It was crated by the lack of information to make an accurate prediction.

It impacts your ability to function and creates a personality trait called NEUROTICISM.

There are different levels of the fear of unknown going from low, moderate and high which translates in terror.

Covid-19 created and exacerbated new level of fear of unknown due to the lack of knowledge, control and predictability.

Avoiding this fear provides temporary relief, but it is detrimental to your health in the long run. It is recommended to start analyzing and taking steps towards finding out more about the unpredictable situation.

By creating tolerance to uncertainty and emotional intelligence, you can have a better understanding of recognizing and accepting your emotions.

Individual, group therapy and medical help are the answers to creating peace of mind.

2. FEAR OF BEING LONELY

Mostly related to age when the older ones lost the loved ones around them.

It is a state of mind related to lack of companionship or separation from the others.

Some of these individuals try to fight loneliness by doing activities or pursuing hobbies, some become very shy, some try to compensate by being around other people.

With age, people seem to lose the ability to make friends or start a new relationship especially if there are some language or ethnic barriers there.

Many times, they end up in isolation and solitude.

3. FEAR OF AGING

It is common in older people most of them retired or close to it with no major goals, plans, activities or hobbies.

It happens to people who are being alone with no resources to survive or depending on someone intellectually or physically.

4. FEAR OF MEMORY LOSS

Again, we are talking about older people, women in menopause or people suffering from Alzheimer disease.

They can remember things that happened moments ago, phone numbers or anything related to short memory.

They have problems with long-term memory, repressing thoughts that are considered unnecessary; this leads to guilt and anxiety.

5. FEAR OF BEING ALONE

It happens to people with guilty consciousness or vacant minds.

They isolate themselves from the family or society but in the same time they crave company.

6. FEAR OF BEING ONESELF

Some individuals tend to mirror the lives of their same-sex parents, mostly women, who were raised to be the image of their mothers. They grow under domineering parents with great expectations and this feeling is perpetuating to their children too.

7. FEAR OF LOVE AND COMMITMENT

It is common in people coming from broken families, abusive fathers or bitter love relationship that ended in a heartbreak, divorce or worse.

Looking on the bright side, LOVE is a strong emotion worth fighting for.

Love is trust, respect, acceptance, tenderness, sexual pleasure, devotion but also taking risks.

People can go into a state of **PHILOPHOBIA**, which is literally fear of love.

8. SEXUAL FEARS

It is an impaired erotic response to sexual partners.

It might refer to the impossibility of men in having an erection, premature ejaculation or the size of the penis.

This is a vicious circle and the more they fear the poorly they perform.

It can also be related to trivial cultural situations like forbidding masturbation or, even worse, the abuse and molestation in the past. It will lead to impotence of frigidity or the necessity to use bizarre objects like fetishes.

9. FEAR OF REJECTION

It is associated with social phobias and means the fear of being excluded or criticized.

People in this category become shy, avoid meeting other people, have a low self-esteem and consider that **THEY ARE NOT GOOD ENOUGH**.

This is related to fear of failing, fear of betrayal, and fear of taking chances.

10. FEAR OF CRITICISM

The individuals become reluctant to do any activities at home or work and they are scared of confrontations considering that they have been manipulated.

It leads to low self-esteem and it is very much related to the fear of rejection.

11. FEAR OF TAKING RISKS

It is the fear of taking decisions that implies taking a risk of making errors.

Those people prefer the safety of their home or known places or situations and avoid investments or stock market.

12. FEAR OF ABANDONMENT

Most common in children because their parents threaten to send them away as a disciplinary measure.

Some are removed and placed in foster homes or live with relatives.

In adults, the fear is generated by being dependent on someone else or by the loss of power.

It is a state of anticipation related with fear of being lonely and creates severe anxieties.

13. FEAR OF HOMELESSNESS

Common in people with mental disorders or financial issues.

They become alcoholics, drug abusers, rapists, or end up being detained by the police. According to professionals, this category of adults or children should benefit from government care (food, overnight shelter, transportation medical care).

Churches often provide emergency or long time care.

14. FEAR OF DISEASES (hypochondria)

It is the preoccupation with having multiple serious diseases based on the interpretation of a physical sign or sensation.

It persists even after medical assurance and it is mostly an exaggeration of a mild condition.

People suffering from this condition show anxiety, depressions and compulsive behavior.

15. FEAR OF HELL

It materializes in the fear of burning in the underworld because of a sinful life.

Religion aspects created it and it serves as a disciplinary method for the people who have too much pleasure in life or seek to harm the others.

The punishment is orchestrated by the DEVIL, the personification of the DEMON, even in a world ruled by GOD.

15. FEAR OF GOD

16. FEAR OF DEATH

I consider these last two subjects very important for the human beings and I will take more time and space to talk about them.

Fear Of God

WE FEAR MEN SO MUCH BECAUSE WE FEAR GOD SO LITTLE.

WILLIAM GURNALL

WHY DO WE FEAR GOD?

THE FEAR OF LORD IS THE BEGGING OF WISDOM

PROVERB 9:10

When we think about the FEAR of GOD, we associate this feeling with the religion and its manipulations to keep people under control otherwise God will turn his back on us and we will end up in Hell.

The real and valid interpretation of the fear of God is a reverent feeling for His power, the submission and acknowledgment of His love and lordship.

We stand in awe in front of God because there is nothing to fear, there is only love and God is love.

We should obey His commands not out of fear but because they are the proper ones and He has the infinite power to answer our prayers.

Just by serving Lord and Master will make our fears disappear.

In the presence of God we should become courageous because He is with us all the time, protecting and loving us all.

It is time for the misunderstanding of the fear of God to make room for reflection and finding the essence of His commands.

CAN WE BE FRIENDS WITH GOD?

YOU WILL SEEK ME AND FIND ME WHEN YOU SEEK ME WITH ALL YOUR HEART.

JEREMIAH 29:13

God created the humans to be his friends.

Like any friendship it requires time together, conversation, communication and action.

WE long to be with Him, in His presence all the time.

The Hebrew word for "presence" is "face".

We are commanded to seek God's face and His energy not only when we have problems but all the time with prayers and offerings.

THE PRESENCE OD GOD IS LIFE AND JOY, PEACE PURPOSE, FORGIVENESS, WHOLENESS AND UNCONDITIONAL LOVE.

Without Him we become hungry and thirsty in a spiritual way, in our hearts.

We have to break our daily routine, look around and seek and feel God's presence at any given moment.

It is never too late. Remember that Moses was eighty years old when God spoke to him through a burning bush.

We seek His presence and we become hungry for more.

Tozer says, "You have as much of God as you want".

When you practice feeling His presence, you and people around will notice a big change in you.

You will feel His protection, His peace and your fears will turn into gratefulness.

Praising and worshiping God will be your war against fear and anxiety.

Friendship with God feels like home because God wants to make a home with you, to dwell with you and to rest with you.

BEHOLD THE DWELLING PLACE OF GOD IS WITH MEN.
HE WILL DWELL WITH THEM AND THEY WILL BE HIS PEOPLE AND GOD HIMSELF WILL BE WITH THEM AS THEIR GOD. (REVELATION 21:3)

He will dwell in our hearts and will be with us forever as a guide, friend and helper.

In the difficult times of covid, God showed us the path to peace and rest.

We should obey his rules as if the children obey their Father in order to build a relationship based on love.

Eventually this big friendship will please Lord and you together.

THE POWER OF PRAYER

SO I PRAYED TO THE GOD OF HEAVEN. (NEHEMIAH 2:4)

We are all becoming children when comes to asking for help and we try to imagine a supernatural force looking for us from above.

Prayers have a corresponding blessing connected with it.

We have expectations when we pray from the heart; we let our prayers out to be heard or we pray in silence but ultimately we all seek comfort.

There is a notion that a prayer is a very simple thing, a short business that can be done without care or effort.

Some people think that if they keep the Bible on the night table and go through some passages in a rush it is enough to please God.

A prayer needs a preparation.

Look at the priest preparing for a prayer: he will wear a nice suit or regalia, will wash his hands and will take some time for reflections as they come from a supreme force.

Prayer is a ritual and should be done with holly carefulness.

It is not only the kneeling but also the preparation to carry and worship God's word.

We pray to a God that we cannot hear and see but His divine presence requires humbleness and trust.

We cannot expect to solve our problems with a prayer but ask for mercy and accept the gift of grace.

Pray from your fervent heart, pray until you can pray. Pray to be help to pray, use simple words and make an art out of a simple prayer.

The very act of prayers is a blessing, is easing your burdens, tear down your disappointments and fill your body with vigor and hope.

You will glorify God and the world will be moved and will be filled with love.

Praying makes us the recipient of receiving the honor of being with God, receive his love and favors; we should approach it with great submission.

We pray loud or we whisper...

His hand is outstretched to search for all of us no matter where you are, in a cab, at work or a place of worship.

A prayer is good for the heart, for your moral, for your confidence, for your memory, for your wellbeing and good mood.

The prayer can be long or brief and concise like LORD HELP ME; that moment is a moment of bliss.

A prayer is not measured by its length but by its sincerity and intensity.

When you witness a miracle don't ask yourself "Am I not lucky?" but say "Lord, make it a real blessing for me".

Reading the Bible is not an information but a transformation.

It is not a book of rules but the path to build a relationship with God.

Reading it without practicing the commands doesn't make any sense, it is a waste of time and will deceive you and God.

Not feeling the Bible when you read it is like reading a note from a friend or loving father and then throwing it in the garbage or simply ignore it.

I don't believe that there is any human being out there not thinking of the existence of a supreme force named God or otherwise ruling the Universe.

I have a confession to make: it was not easy for me to write this last chapter without a deep study of the Bible and a lot of time for reflection.

As I mentioned before, I was brought up in a country where religion and prayers were forbidden. As a child I portrayed God as a Santa Klaus dressed in white, directing dead people to the right (Heaven) or to the left (Hell).

After I fled my country I started to shape my beliefs so today I can call myself a "universal believer".

I witnessed miracles myself.

I was visiting the Pueblo native people from Santa Fe and I went to a house of prayer called Sanctuario de Chimayo in the middle of nowhere.

I don't recall seeing a priest or an altar but two rooms, one for kids and one for adults filled with discarded crutches or glasses.

In the middle of one room, there was a hole in the ground filled with sand and everybody was taking away a cup full of it.

They said that the sand has healing powers and it has to be rubbed on the body or brewed in the tea.

There were thousands of people taking sand away but the hole was always full…

When I traveled to Peru, I experienced the force of the spiritual vortex of the Earth and I bought a crystal that I use in my prayers.

I pray a lot… I pray in joy, in sorrow, in sickness and distress.

I say prayers, I whisper mantras and I meditate.

I am in awe with the power of the Moon and the Sun and I am enchanted by the Nature's superb geometry in creating a butterfly wing.

I bow thinking of the miracle of Death and Life, the anatomy of a simple cell, the complexion of the human DNA and the infinite of the Universe.

I believe that human beings were put here for a reason and not due to evolution; we have a special gene that is not found in any other living creature. I am fascinated by quantum physics but also by old Indian and Native approaches to existence.

But until we discover those miracles let's enjoy a prayer with reverence, make peace and find bliss in our heart and our souls and venerate a common God that looks upon everybody with love.

I will end this chapter with some powerful highlights that I cherish from the book 'Conversation with God" by Neale Donald Walsch:

Be your shining example.

Make every moment from your life an outpouring of love.

Be a living, breathing example of the highest truth that resides within you.

Make of your life a gift."

Thank you!

GOD AND REALITY

GOD is in trouble!

FAITH must be saved!

When we have a down moment, we ask ourselves if God did something for us lately and instead of keeping the faith, we turn the back to God.

If God exists, why is there so much suffering in the world?

Should we really surrender or just walk away from FAITH?

People losing their faith lose actually their love.

Faith has to be restored because without it we lose the passion for eternal and the mystery of existence.

Unbelief is when we refuse to accept that GOD is real; faith is when we hope that GOD is real.

Knowledge is the acceptance of the reality of God's existence.

We believe in God because we need to feel safe, loved and protected.

GOD drives us to achieve, create, become inspired and nonjudgmental.

He will help us bond with the loved ones, fact that is one of the most important need to survival.

In the ultimate state of unity, God is us. We become one and we reach the goal of seeking the truth. We become centered, deeper connected with ourselves, and we merge with the SOURCE.

All is forgiven, all is loved.

Unfortunately, faith can also come with strong emotional negative attachments and being expressed in this wrong way will be very harmful.

The FANATICISM practiced by some Muslims is a blind fate that rewards the suicide bombers with the gift or receiving virgins in heaven if they complete their mission.

Einstein was struggling with his orthodox Jewishness when he realized that the loss of faith could be devastating for the humanity.

He was more interested in the essence and completeness of the faith than practicing any religion.

We go through faith and non-faith.

Sometimes we feel that God didn't respond to our prayers and he failed us.

We get angry when God does not show us mercy, love and comfort and we become skeptical about His existence.

When God comes and goes, judges, demands or abandons us He becomes an illusion.

True FAITH is when we believe in ourselves, allow our bodies and minds to heal, bond with our loved ones, and have faith in progress and the future. With true faith, we can overcome fear, solve conflicts, fix the troubles and speak the truth.

God is in all things and is only loving, good, peaceable and just.

He doesn't have an ego, he likes what you like, he is generous and approves your actions.

Going through a material world is seeing the light and darkness, the good and evil.

Than you reach a transitional world when white and black emerge and become gray and you become more aware.

Last step is transcendental world where we reach a state of unity, love and bliss.

When you touch the highest state of awareness, you feel light, safe, still, accepting, forgiving, true and fearless.

If you want to know God, you have to change.

You want a better life, you are curious and wise and you experience a higher self.

You just need an everyday motivation not a hand on your shoulder or an extra mystical voice.

Than we have the "AHA" moments, all is clear, peaceful, wonderful, inspired, guided, the energy is falling in place.

God is you, pure awareness, creativity, possibility, bliss, balance, guidance, whole.

From the nonalignment, which is disorder, you go to alignment, which is peace.

God allows you to remember, forgive and forget, offers you a world of possibilities, helps you overcome separation and isolation.

He gives you the greatest gift by offering you a new world of possibilities.

Redefine yourself in a multidimensional life and escape the traps of the physical world through faith.

HOW DO WE REACH THE STATE OF EXPERIENCING GOD?

Meditate in silence, observe and face the truth, be mindful, compassionate and let go of materialism.

See that not everything in life is permanent, even life itself is temporary.

Reexamine your present situation, think about your friends, family, career, hobbies, politics, travel, charity.

Reflect on your stress level.

Pray, silence your mind, reevaluate your state of grace and your gratitude.

Free your consciousness, escape the previous state of denial and search for the hidden meaning of everyday events.

Identify yourself with your HIGHER SELF.

Become generous in love, actions and spirit.

Take a deep breath and let go of the greed, selfishness, fear, loss, contradictions, resistance.

SURRENDER!

Center yourself before you act, react, and open yourself to acceptance.

Change the routine, evolve and be satisfied by retraining your brain.

HEAL!

Give your body the equilibrium through contentment.

Raise your expectations to an unlimited potential, erase your doubts and fears.

Find the happiness within you not in the glamour of Ritz or Chanel.

Let it be and the solutions will appear out of nowhere.

God is reality and consciousness.

My beloved mentor Deepak Chopra said:
"If God is the creator force of everything,
And God is within us,
The creative force of everything is in us"

FAITH IS FEARLESSNESS!

GOD IS WITH US

What do we do when we cannot face the reality and we fear about tomorrow?

The fear can be exhausting, can wipe us out, burn the energy within us and hinder us from experiencing the presence of God.

Fear can take away our hope of life, the love, spontaneity and the fun we have within ourselves.

Life is a gift of God to be enjoyed without fear.

In the Scripture, God is urging us not to be afraid.

God is not condemning us to feel the fear but he assures us that he loves us and is always with us.

Making the choice to see God near us is very personal.

Trusting Him is a process with stages and it comes bit by bit.

There are also times when God keeps us in the dark because He is the reason to keep us waiting.

Eventually we will see that more light and feel more love and we will have the courage and trust to take the next step.

Sometimes God does not confirm the way we follow the steps in faith. He is bigger than we see and will reveal Himself even in our disappointments and disillusionment.

Growing in our trust is a long personal process and the more we trust Him, the more He is with us.

We will feel His presence in our life and will develop a close relationship with Him.

We can experience God's presence by turning to him inwardly and cultivating an awareness of Him.

God will show in our life unexpectedly; we cannot control Him.

We can enter His presence or He can just show up and make Himself known.

Like a father and a friend He is LOVE, WISDOM, PEACE, MERCY, SALVATION; He is there exactly when we need Him.

Being in His presence is always an emotional experience and he gives us a chance to believe in Him regardless of the emotions that we feel.

His promise is "I am with you".

The more we trust Him the more we experience emotions and the more we step and believe the more we feel His presence.

We can experience his presence through His creation; it is either a beautiful bird or a breathtaking sunset.

Alternatively, we can feel Him through the people around us that support us.

When a good friend prays for us in a difficult time in our life God is telling us that He is near.

We feel at ease in His presence, we feel comfort and reassurance... it is like falling in love.

God wants to touch us in different ways, He wants to cradle us and soothe us.

He will be with us today, tomorrow, every day.

Our desperation and pain will become His opportunity to meet with us, to identify with us and to walk us to another level of intimacy and trust.

Whatever you do or feel God sees you, knows your situation, and hears your prayers...He is just there with you.

When we surrender to God, we release our weakness and we gain freedom.

Don't hesitate to ask for His help even if you feel unworthy, you have a mess in your life or you feel beyond help.

He is eager to be called for help because He is with us and our inner peace comes from Him.

The former South African President F. W. Klerk, in his Nobel Price acceptance speech said:

"The greatest peace I believe is the peace that we derive from our faith in God Almighty, from certainty from our relationship with our Creator.

Crises might beset us, battles might rage about us but if we have faith and the certainty it brings, we will enjoy peace, the peace that surpasses all understanding".

If we lack peace in our hearts, we have to stop and pray.

If you lack direction in your life, turn to God and ask more questions.

Peace and answers will come to you.

When we are still, we can tune into what God is speaking to our hearts and minds; centering on God brings us peace.

It is not up to us to achieve peace.

Peace is what He is and He enables us to rest in His presence.

God's invitation to be with Him is not a command but a graceful way to fill us with Him.

Embracing God's forgiveness is an act of faith, a process of growth and can take some time.

His forgiveness is purely unconditional love and God wants us to love and enjoy life; it is a gift to enjoy.

We are here to tell others about how God helped us as a sign of faith and hope.

It is about His abilities, His consistency and His love.

God will give us a purpose and will empower us to fulfill all our responsibilities that He places in our hands.

Learning about life with God today will help you build a better tomorrow.

We all hope in a better future; this is the deep desire in our heart.

The Bible says" And now these three remain: faith, hope and love" (Corinthians 13:13 NIV)

God is our today and our tomorrow, he has work to do today and will be there with us.

Fear Of Death

THOSE WHO FEAR DEATH MOST ARE THOSE
WHO ENJOY LIFE LEAST.

EDWARD ABBEY

Fear of DEATH is one of the most common fears and it is associated with many phobias.

"Scared to death" is a very common term and it is used by individuals who are so frightened by circumstances that they will fear until they die.

Because of the unknown side of death, the religion incorporated the fear of death into the belief system.

Many people still believe that death is painful and unpleasant especially because they lose contact with the loved ones still alive.

In US people don't use the word DIE or DEATH but they rather refer to it as "passing away".

Many cultures believe that DEATH is a stage of life, a part of the WHEEL OF LIFE and the dead people become spirits and accompany the living ones.

Fear of death is present in people of all ages but mostly in the older ones who live alone.

As part of the defense mechanism, the soldiers in wars learn to control or suppress fear of death in order to become efficient in combat.

There are two distinct categories when talking about the fear of death.
One refers to the fear of losing someone loved through the process of dying, the other is the fear of our own death.

Most of the people when they face their own death or someone's death go through a deep process of suffering called GRIEF.

GRIEF

It is the same process for the terminally ill patients as well as the family and the loved ones who witness the death of a sick patient, most of the time happening in the same time.
Elisabeth Gilbert speaks about the grief:

"Grief doesn't obey our plans or our wishes.
Grief will do whatever it wants to you whenever it wants to.
In that regard grief has a lot in common with love.
It doesn't mean that we are sad for the rest of our life.
Give grief a final place."

David Kessler says:

"Each person's grief is as unique as a fingerprint.
But what everyone has in common is that no matter how they grieve they share the need of grief to be shared."

We feel the loss of what could be the loss of what we know and understand about a situation or a person.
We feel lost and we need to reassess every part of our emotional, physical and social worlds.
People struggle with the fear that their story and their grief will not be validated.
This is why people grieving need support healing groups with people going through similar experience.

Grief can be cause by the loss of a close friend, a spouse, a child, a parent, a pet or even a job.

It is followed by a process of MOURNING.

The renowned psychologist Elisabeth Kubler-Ross identifies the stages of grief as very important and necessary steps to bring the process to a resolution and closure.

For some it might take hours, days, years; some might experience the stages in the order listed or not, back and forth, skip emotions or process the whole thing totally different or skipping voluntarily the grieving out of fear of broken heart.

STAGES OF GRIEF

1. DENIAL

We cannot believe that the person has died and we carry on numb, like nothing happened.

We believe that the dead person will come back because we feel her presence around.

The dying people deny that they have to die.

2. ANGER

We judge the death as unfair and cruel.

We get angry with the dead or with yourself for not doing enough to keep that person alive.

3. BARGAINING

We start making deals we ourselves or with God, going over the event and asking questions like "What if?"

We wish to go back in time and change things in the hope that we will feel differently.

This step is powerful and goes hand in hand with guilt.

4. DEPRESSION

When we realize the reality of death we become overwhelmed by sadness and pain; the emotions come in waves and culminate with the thought that life doesn't make sense anymore.

5. ACCEPTANCE

This is already the stage when the process of healing starts.

The pain eases and the acceptance of the facts sips in.

We may not go over the grieving process totally but we start to learn how to live with the memories.

The whole process is sometimes very long and hard, requires a lot of energy and people get so fatigued that they isolate themselves.

But there are ways to alleviate the pains of grieving.

First you acknowledge your pain and seek emotional support with people who care about you or you seek medical help.

Taking care of yourself will help you and the others recover from the loss.

Sometimes when the grief is not consumed at the right time, it can hit you unexpectedly, months or years after the death of a loved one; it is called "the delayed grief".

This is why, for a variety of reasons, it is not advisable to conceal your emotions. Better yet, feel your pain, cherish the memories of the beloved ones so that you can come to closure and start the healing process.

Watching a loved one dying is not easy even though the cessation of the functions of the body is not painful or frightening.

"Watching a peaceful death of a human being reminds us of a falling star; one of a million lights in a vast sky that flares up for a brief moment only to disappear into the endless night forever".

Elisabeth Kubler-Ross

FEARING OUR DEATH

Deepak Chopra says "DEATH ENDED NOTHING; IT OPENED A LIMITLESS ADVENTURE".

It is said that when we are alive, we are like a river flowing in one direction to the ocean; when we die, we become a cloud and we have no direction.

The concept of death is so different and personal and is heavily influenced by family beliefs, religion and culture.

In addition, the experience of death is the same for all religions, Aboriginal from Australia, Hindu, Muslims, Christians, and Atheists.

It doesn't depend on age or economic or political status.

The subject of death is taboo for many cultures.

We feel perhaps only subconsciously to be in contact with death in any way we can make it more real or thinkable.

In THE ILIAD Homer, calls sleep "death sister".

In Turkey, there is a graveyard 100.000 years old and possibly used by Neanderthal people; the fossilized imprints have enabled the archaeologists to discover that the men buried their dead on beds of flowers as a celebration of the human spirit survival.

The Muslims envision the Paradise as a garden with HOURIS (virgin women).

The Greeks expect to meet the shades of the departed across the river Styx in Hades, but not the Satan Hades, the Elysian Fields full of blessed spirits.

Aboriginals from Australia have the DREAM TIME as a way to show the total dependence of the spiritual level of life and death.

Japan and China believe in an invisible world.

Native Americans believe in stairs under the ground that lead the dead into another world.

People in Bali celebrate death with color, noise and joy.

They consider life cyclical and the state of mind of the moment is very important for the next journey.

Kadek, one simple man from Bali says that the cremation frees the soul and purifies it and allows the dead to rejoice the cycle of reincarnation.

The cremation of a high Balinese priest is described with very colorful details in the book "In the weeds", written by Tom Vitale.

The body is washed and wrapped in a white cloth before being placed in a pagoda that will transport the deceased into the next life. The whole procession is noisy; a lot of banging of drums, chanting, laughing, all of it resembling a victory.

The noise is off tune in order to reverberate in the body, shattering the illusion between life and death.

The pagoda is set on fire and an additional inflammable liquid is sprayed on the dead body to insure that it is fully burned and already gone to the unseen world.

Ultimately, the burned body is poked with a tool to make sure there is no life left.

Then the friends and family are happy for the freedom of the soul of the departed.

And the list goes on...

"Because it is your life, it is what you make of it.

No, it is not always fair.

No, it is not always good.

It burns, and tears and there are times when it crashes beyond recognition.

Some people fight against it, others can't, thought I don't think they can be blamed for that.

Giving up is easy.

Picking yourself up is not.

But we believe if we do, we can take another step.

We are here to make sure that life is not always about living, there are many parts of it and it continues even after death.

It's beautiful even if it hurts". T.J.Klune

Personally, because I was raised in a communist country I didn't grow up reading the Bible.

I studied this subject and I embraced different approaches of death; I firmly believe in the concept of death supported by the Indian culture and the Natives.

One of my beloved mentors, Sadhguru, is presenting the death concept in a very easy to understand way.

DEATH has three components: biological, psychological and metaphysical.

We have a clear understanding about how biologically life begins and ends.

But why life and death happen is still little understood.

Death is a fundamental question and people avoid the concept most likely believing in stories spread by their religion.

160.000 people die every single day because we don't have a permanent lease on life.

Death is not a calamity but religion or other ignorant people fictionally create a tragedy like it; it is just moving to another dimension of Existence.

The human's perception about life is that someone has to bleed or breathe.

In reality, death means going from a dynamic form to an inert one.

We know that everything around us is alive...the plants, the cosmic space, our soul.

Even the water is alive and has a memory and intelligence.

The question is: ARE WE ALIVE ENOUGH TO PERCEIVE IT?

The explanatory definition of death is the absence of life but we don't have a definition of life so far.

People die a clinical death, somatic death, but when they come back to life, they create a lot of chaos in this subject.

The English language doesn't diagnose someone as dead but declares him dead because he doesn't respond to a stimulus anymore.

The disembodiment is a slow process and goes in stages and the spiritual life of the body still stays for a while.

CROSSING OVER for the people who experience a clinical death means that they can see themselves leaving the physical body and looking down but they are unable to talk.

By crossing over, the body stops working and it becomes lighter.
The real physical world vanishes but the mind continues to operate.

Personality fades and the feeling of "I" goes to a divine phase of Existence.

As long as we have the power of awareness and an open mind, we can integrate the concept of the life after death in our reality.
The ultimate goal is to fuse with goodness, God and yourself.
The trapping of existence can fall anytime while the essence of life will remain.

'We are here to make sure that life is not always about living.
There are many parts of it and it continues even after death.
It is beautiful even if it hurts." (T. J. Klune)

Because it is your life, make the most of it even if it hurts or crushes you or if it is not always so good.
Giving up is easy, but without it we cannot take another step.
We cannot interfere with death; you start dying from the moment you are born.
Yes, you live, breathe, love, ache but you also die.
Death is cleansing and the end of mortal pain.
Death is THE GIFT!

DON'T DISTURB THE DEAD!

Disturbed souls can be caught between the two worlds.

We are advised not to call the dead through prayers, or get in touch with them through different occult practices; they have to go peacefully into the womb of Mother Earth.

The sleeping soul is surrounded by a cocoon of high frequency that can lead them to their loved ones because love is vibration itself. When the body tunes into the frequency of the loved ones on a physical level the persons alive can feel the presence of the departed.

In India someone can die after learning and reaching maximum evolution; he just dies at his will (usually monks or yogis) leaving behind just a puddle of water.

Death is not a miracle but it brings miraculous things; it brings timelessness, goes beyond boundaries of space and reveals the source of life transforming you into a child of eternity.

Respect death as we respect love, truth and compassion.

PREPARE FOR DEATH

Moving from a physical to a nonphysical state could be the greatest movement of your life and we have to make it gracefully.

People who lived an accomplished joyful life are not afraid of death.

Once your body runs its course you will die even if you want or not. This is why taking care of our body while we are alive is so important.

Still we fear death...we have insecurities and lack of education.

HOW TO DIE

We all die...surprise, surprise!

Sooner or later, we die a forced death, a sudden death, or an arranged death. Religion and culture influences very much the way we die, how we die and when we die.

Some cultures don't allow the cross over event to be decided...unless it happens suddenly due to accidents, war or illness.

Many people wait until their bodies are so worn out and old, hoping to wake up to another day just to breathe; they might undergo expensive and complicated medical procedures to make the agony last longer, regardless of poor life quality. Some others with debilitating conditions turn into advocates to support life no matter the body state.

Some with damaged mind or body beyond repair chose suicide... just leave them alone!

The modern medicine is against death especially by suicide and actually, for every annual checkup you have to complete a form about thoughts of suicide.

If you agree that you have dark thoughts, you are immediately sent to a psychiatrist for tons of medication, to counseling or hospice.

REINCARNATION

The reincarnation process is very common and discussed in Indian culture.

The origin of this theory is THEOSOPHY, a movement that grew in the nineteenth century, based on ideas from Indian Philosophy.

The writer James S. Perkins approached and explained the subject in his book "Experiencing Reincarnation".

The reincarnation is a process of complete surrender but still having the freedom of choice to shape and control your own karma.

Reincarnation allows a soul to experience the Heaven and Hell from previous life until MOKSA (liberation) is achieved.

It creates a gap in the memory that is carried from one life to another while we remain the same but better shaped.

This is how consciousness becomes new and can never be destroyed.

The Tibetan monks have a book called "The Tibetan Book" where they explain reincarnation as a gift for a better Heaven and a better next life.

This book was written in the eighth century A.D., but it was kept hidden and unknown to outsiders. The book was written as related to the funeral ceremony of the dying person during the closing moments of his life.

First was the intent to help a dying person to keep in mind the nature of the phenomenon.

Second was to help the people still alive to not hold into dying and think positive.

In "the rebirth of Lamas", we hear stories but some speculate that this are just legends to increase the reputation of the monastery.

Among Tibetans, one life is connected to another, and so the reincarnated persons (especially Lamas) will not break the chain of identity.

Only when the soul has unfinished business they reincarnate and continue a task from a previous life, or in the case of a Guru continues to teach the disciples.

People should dig into their past only for spiritual reasons, because most of they cannot handle the memories and emotions of a lifetime.

The opening of the past cannot bring any good but people insist on going there through different occult ways or hypnosis.

We experience the Deja-vu but we still ask ourselves:
Will I come back?
We don't know when our expiration date will come or if we still have unpaid debts to pay in a next life.

CREMATION

This approach has lately been much more embraced by people for different reasons. The idea of cremation is that there is nothing left behind after the physical body dies...so when you are gone you are gone.

The body should disappear and not let rot by the forces of brutal nature.

The Indians add salt and turmeric to the dead before cremation to speed up the process of dissolving the body.

They also tie the big toes of the dead together so that the outside energy from the outside world is not sucked back into the body, depleting or disturbing the living people.

The Indians die in KASHI (the cremation ground), which is built in the city and on the river Ganga.

The process of cremation is a continuous ritual 24 hour a day every day and people cremated and sent to flow on the Ganga river are supposed to have a happy death.

The fire in Kashi is supposed to burn forever from the beginning of time to the eternity and many families keep the flame alive from generation to generation.

Even with the cremation the real death and crossing over is a slow process because the movement to a new realm is yet not happening for a while.

No matter how many cremations take place the river Ganga is holly and people wash themselves there, drink water from it and pray together without any fear of pollution.

The poet Rumi says, "Death is our wedding to eternity".

EUTHANASIA

Is euthanasia a crime or a gift?

It is called "Mercy Killing" and it is supposed to be the death solution for the terminal illness.

Unfortunately, this procedure is not accepted in many countries (only Belgium, Luxembourg, the Netherlands and Colombia).

There are several types of euthanasia: active, passive, indirect, physician assisted suicide.

Also we have voluntary euthanasia when the patient requests it or involuntary when the patient is incompetent to take decisions.

The American pathologist Jack Kevorkian dedicated his life to respect and preserve the right of euthanasia in US but unfortunately because of different restrictions he was accused of crimes against humanity and imprisoned.

At least he helped 130 people die with decency and dignity.

Again I come with a very personal opinion: the way we choose the death of our beloved out of mercy to end their suffering should be considered, we should let people choose their death when they have no hope to recover or they live a life in pain.

We should remember and honor the dead but not in extreme.

People build monuments to honor the loved ones who are gone but unfortunately, all those things turn into a moneymaker touristic attraction where the visitors don't mourn the death but admire the architecture of the building (Taj Mahal built in the memory of princess Mumtaz)

Egyptians pyramids are another example but it is known that the shape of the pyramid is meant to preserve the physical body for long time after death.

Native Americans leave the bodies to the birds, and the ground is sacred and is not to be disturbed by the living.

Every person is unique in their beliefs and the very thought that life is not forever is very scary.

Some people age and mourn differently because of different factors and limitations.

However, we are all bound in a field of consciousness beyond our bodies, in our home beyond the stars. Without death, we cannot be present in the moment because the last moment has to die before a next moment is possible.

There is no love until the last emotion dies and let another love blossom.

There is no present life in our body until some of the old cells die and new tissue is born.

The biggest miracle of life and death is their continuous dance.

We should look at our cosmic live in the infinite Universe without doubt or fear.

I should end this beautiful chapter with a verse of Tagore:
"AND BECAUSE I LOVE THIS LIFE I WILL LOVE DEATH AS WELL."

THE MYSTERY OF DEATH
(Clinical death)

When do we know that a person is dead?

1. Absence of clinical detectable vital signs.
2. Absence of brain activity.
3. Irreversible loss of vital functions.

We reached an era in our society when we need to have the courage to have an open mind to new areas of research about the subject of death.

I, myself was closed to death several times but I cannot claim the objectivity based on an after death experience.

I have no proof that this can happen after a clinical death and I hope that I don't offend anybody by touching this subject, nor do I try to convince anybody to accept or believe the content of my affirmation.

Dying is a process as normal as any other process; it is almost identical with birth into a new existence.

It is not only a matter of belief but also a matter of knowing the things concerning what lays beyond.

Human concern with the nature of death is universal, and any light that can be shed on the nature of death is very welcome. This kind of enlightenment should be taught by members of many professional and academic fields.

This would have very profound implications for every one of us in understanding life and death.

An enormous mass of information still lies in the mind of the persons who experience life after death but they refuse to talk about it out of fear of being labeled crazy or over imaginative.

On the other hand, this field is not really explored by physicians, who are likely to hear most of the near-death experiences after resuscitating the patients.

Dr. Raymond Moody, in his book "Life after life" talks about people's experience before being resuscitated from a clinical death.

Most of them experience a paranormal episode.

All those persons reported seeing a light or being the light in a wide variety of unusual setting.

Others experience a pleasant feeling, the space as a void, a vacuum in the shape of a cylinder or hear a music of some sort.

Others describe some floating sensation, a feeling of weightlessness as an awareness of physical sensation of body weight, movement or position.

One woman, as per Dr. Moody describes the life after death like a blessing in a way that makes life more precious; she looked toned, with a better attitude and wished to enjoy the present life.

Going back to one of my favorite people, Elisabeth Kubler-Ross, a remarkable medical doctor, psychiatrist, and tanologist, she makes herself the guinea pig of this experiment. She gives herself a self-death induction in order to experience an out of body experience session; she explains that she felt an unusual speed and detachment from the physical body, looking back at it.

When she came back she was radiating, looking younger and in a perfect state of health.

What she felt is called cosmic consciousness; it is merging with spiritual energy and the source of life and peace that will erase all the agonies, pains and sorrows that we have endured in life.

She did the death induction and she claims that only due to this experience she felt the urge of harmony between the physical, emotional and spiritual quadrants and the importance of fulfilling the destiny.

The reward of this experiment was very fulfilling and created a lot of buzz in the medical field.

She explained in her book ON DEATH AND DYING her experience with the terminally ill patients with fear of death, and speaks about convincing the patients to embrace death with courage and dignity.

After going through all the stages of grief that we talked about earlier the patient and the loved ones around him should reach acceptance as a final stage before the great journey.

Death should come as a relief, as a detachment from the sick body.

It is very important to speak with the sick people about death and dying as a normal process like birth and the importance of going through all the stages of grief together with all the members of the family.

Sometimes the outsiders hold on to someone's life and refuse to separate; it creates chaos in the last moments of the ill patient who cannot find peace and acceptance and die in silence and bliss.

Elisabeth Kubler-Ross's goal in her practice is to help patients and family overcome the crisis together and achieve the moment of acceptance.

She tells the story of one patient who was afraid of death because of fear of darkness and worms.

She talks to the family about the option of cremation and as soon as the patient heard about the alternative, she died immediately in peace.

Because life is so short, in the spam of our existence, we should live and love more.

We should learn not to fear and open all the channels of the mind.

Everything about life is positive and death is just as positive with a hint of challenge.

The process of death is similar with what happens with a butterfly emerging from a cocoon.

The cocoon is similar to the human body where we live for a while.

Dying is moving from the temporary house into a more beautiful one, which is permanent.

As soon as the cocoon becomes irreparable and impossible to come back to, the butterfly emerges and experiences the transformation that can teach us how to embrace death without fear.

It is also like putting away the winter coat when the spring comes.

You are in the possession of awareness and knowledge and you will remember any moment you experienced in a human life.

"Death how is it not fair?

You are born, yes.

You live, breathe, and dance and ache, but you die. Everyone does.

Death is cleansing; the pain of a mortal life is gone.

We don't interfere with death.

We can't.

Because it is always there, no matter what we do, what kind of life we live, good or bad or somewhere in between, it is always going to be waiting for you.

From the moment you are born you are dying". (T.J.Klune.)

DEATH BELONGS TO LIFE AS BIRTH DOES.(Tagore)

Fears Versus Phobias

BE FEARLESS, BE BRAVE, BE BOLD, LOVE
YOURSELF.

HARUKI MURAKAMI

The primary difference between a normal fear and a chronic phobia is that the phobia becomes irrational and impedes the individuals to live a normal life.

The intensity of a phobia is much stronger than just the reaction to fear.

Aaron Beck Md explains in detail the difference between fear and phobia in the book called "Anxiety, disorders and phobias; a cognitive prospective".

One of the key quality that makes a fear into phobias is the magnification of the amount of risk in a situation and the degree of harm that will come from being in that situation.

Because of the greater hazard the phobic person develops a great anxiety but also a greater desire to avoid it.

People dominated by fears and phobias develop nervous habits and behaviors like facial tics and twitches, nail biting or nose picking.

As a result, the defense mechanism of the body comes on stage either useful or harmful depending on the severity of the situation.

Sigmund Freud used and explained the term of defense mechanism like a reaction of the body in form of avoidance, compensation, denial, displacement, repression.

Fears and phobias in children are related to their age and are reaction to pain, loud noises, separation from the parents or starting school.

SYMPTOMS OF FEAR AND PHOBIAS

1. Feelings of dizziness and disconnections from reality.
2. Tingling hands and feet because your blood flows redirected to your muscles, which are more critical to survival.
3. Blurred or altered vision because the pupils dilate in order to perceive more danger.
4. Difficulty concentrating due to decreased blood flow to the brain because the blood flow is redirected.
5. Increasing sweating and cooling the body so you don't overheat.
6. Upset stomach.
7. Difficulty breathing (hyperventilation)
8. Heart racing (sending blood to the vital organs)
9. Feeling shaky due to the release of adrenaline.

Fears and phobias crate different acute or chronic conditions of the body like the following:

ANXIETY

It is a very unpleasant feeling triggered by the anticipation of danger.
It is caused by thoughts (internal) or environment (external).
The name comes from the Latin root "anxious", meaning disturbed or uneasy.

Anxiety relates to a situation or person that the individual has already come to fear through learned experience.

It comes with loneliness, helplessness, and the idea that the world is a hostile place.

The American Psychology Association defines anxiety as "an emotion characterized by feelings of tension, worried thoughts and physical change like increased blood pressure."

Approximately one third of US adults are affected by anxiety but very little seek professional help, which sometimes makes the situation even more complicated.

Anxiety means unnecessary emotional energy consumed and goes hand in hand with fear, so instead of dismissing it we should understand and learn how to deal with anxiety.

The burden of adaptation to anxiety becomes STRESS.

STRESS

It is the disturbance and dis-balance of the wellbeing of the body (homeostasis) leading to symptoms from light to life threatening ones.

It is the internal response to circumstances known as STRESSORS.

Stressors can be personal (illness, finding no pleasure in life or not getting along with people).

It can be work related or environmental.

If it persists it can cause severe health issues or even organs damage.

It affects all areas of life and is recognizable through different signals like insomnia, fatigue, sweating, headache, hives, panic and bad temper.

Renne Brenen approaches stress as "We feel stressed when we evaluate environmental demands as beyond our ability to cope successfully."

Stress is overloading and leads to aging and poor behavior and sometimes inability to function because stress is unfolding quicker than our body can handle.

The stress affects family life, work and finances and the impossibility to cope with it turns people into impulsive, worried, pressured or weak ones.

It leads to depression and PTSD.

PTSD (Post Traumatic Stress Disorder)

It is stress caused by traumas in the past (sexual abuse, war).

The individuals show signs of avoidance, painful detachment, decreased interest, restricted affectionate expressions.

Most of the time this condition should be taken care with medical attention.

DEPRESSION

It is an emotional state marked by great sadness, feeling of inferiority and guilt, lethargy and low self-esteem.

It is the leading reason for the disability in US.

When we don't recognize or accept the signs of depressions and in severe cases refuse to see a specialist it can lead to SUICIDE.

Recent researches indicate that the people suffering from depressions have an imbalance in the neurotransmitters in the brain, which are (natural biochemicals) that allow the brain cells to communicate.

When a suicidal thought arises and before the crisis develops, it is necessary to assist the person at that time.

People who cannot cope with depressions should undergo self-help therapy, group therapy and medication.

Depressions are mostly found in people suffering from manic depressions, alcoholism, substance abuse, and schizophrenia.

PANIC ATTACK

It is a strong surge of anxiety and stress with a peak within 10 minutes.

The symptoms include dizziness, difficulty breathing, rubbery legs, palpitations, excessive perspiration and chocking.

It can be easily interpreted as a heart attack and the individual loses his sense of reality. Those attacks alter the people's life and family relationships, they become reclusive and avoid situations that trigger the attack.

They also develop phobias, paranoia, severe insecurities and low self-esteem.

LOW SELF ESTEEM

SELF ESTEEM means not accepting oneself, not liking oneself and not appreciating oneself as self-worth.

Low self-esteem arises when people become anxious comparing themselves with the others by different standards.

Most of them feel inferior intellectually and physically waiting for approval from others.

Low self-esteem also leads to crime, substance abuse and suicidal thoughts and is common in teenagers and young adults.

Other situations like being abused or forced to do immoral things, having an abortion, being overweight, criticized in public trigger a low self-esteem.

It is very important to manage to create a better image of yourself before it leads to difficult situations; it can be achieved in person or in group through counseling. There are the same therapies for fighting fears and phobias.

Each individual is different and each of us have qualities that have to be taken in consideration.

We have to accept ourselves with our fears insecurities and the other issues and try to work to improve our life.

WE ARE ALL UNIQUE AND SPECIAL!

50 Shades Of Phobia

EXPOSE YOURSELF TO YOUR DEEPEST FEARS.
AFTER THAT...YOU ARE FREE.

JIM MORRISON

Phobia is an irrational FEAR that has no voluntary control over the anxiety response and seeks to avoid the causing situation or stimulus.

It is the fear of a person, object, situation or experience and it cannot be explained when it goes out of proportions. The result is the "phobic reaction" or "phobic disorder" and it is different for each individual.

It can start at any age and often is related to a traumatic event, simple or complex, animals, natural phenomenons, internal stimuli or social events.

I chose some examples that are very common in our everyday life.

1. AGORAPHOBIA

The component is the FEAR of FEAR itself and it comes as a combination of fear of public spaces, stores, crowds, public transportation and it is the biggest phobia in US.

The English term comes from the Greek root "agora" meaning market places.

It involves a collection of fears, such as the fear of leaving home, going to church, or going to crowded public places and as a result, the individual avoids social contact and travels for leisure or work. They can impose themselves restrictions and fall victims to marital or social disharmony.

The symptoms are feelings of helplessness, frightening sensations and body state of agitation, loss of control and panic attacks or even heart attacks and death.

The subjects are extremely shy and seek relief in drugs or alcohol.

One efficient treatment is gradually exposing the individual to open places in order to show them that there is no imminent threat.

2. CLAUSTROPHOBIA

It is the fear of closed spaces like subways, tunnels, elevators and other confined spaces.

The word derived from the Latin "claustrum" meaning bolt or lock.

The most common symptom are suffocation and panic attacks.

It is a response to a stimulus and can be avoided with a proper approach like gradually exposing the individual to the situation, like in the case of agoraphobia.

3. FEAR OF DARKNESS (NYCTOPHOBIA)

It is very common in children mostly 2 age old as a response to separation from the parents or the presence of a monster hater.

It is associated with feeling of uncertainty, helplessness, unfamiliarity and it is more aggravated at night.

Many people suffering from the fear of darkness are more comfortable with a night light.

Related is FEAR OF NIGHTMARES and can be rooted in deep emotional conflicts.

4. FEAR OF WATER (AQUAPHOBIA)

It has a lot in common with FEAR OF DROWNING AND DEATH, FEAR OF SWIMMING, and FEAR OF SEEING IMAGINARY BODIES in the water or FEAR OF FLOOD in rainy seasons.

Many children develop this phobia because overly cautious parents teach them to stay away from water because of a great danger.

The term of AQUAPHOBIA was used first by a Roman medical authority named Celsus who advised that the phobic people should be thrown in a tank of water until they drank more than they needed.

It is also common in swimmers and as a result, they will chose to swim just in shallow waters.

5. FEAR OF FLYING (AEROPHOBIA)

Represents a major category of phobias in US and the survey concludes that 25 million Americans suffer from it.

The anticipatory fear is not the fear of planes but the outcome of losing control, being trapped in a confined space or the fear of death by crashing.

Because flying is one of the most common way of transportation for travel or business there are some tips to be considered before flying:

Prepare yourself to fly in advance, visualize yourself enjoying your flight, see the flight as an opportunity to fight fear, relax and think of safely reaching the destination.

Occupy yourself while flying by reading a book, watching a movie or having a computer-based activity.

6. FEAR OF HEIGHTS (ALTOPHOBIA)

This fear considers the visual space very important, for example seeing the stairs while going down.

The individuals are scared to look down a window, look up, cross a bridge and they start crawling instead of walking.

It is very close related to fear of flying.

7. FEAR OF MOTION (KINESOPHOBIA)

Motion is a strong stimulus that can create the fear of motion.

People in this category fear the speed, racecars, planes, and trains because of the danger that can be involved.

They develop motion sickness together with other symptoms like vomiting and dizziness.

More prone to this condition are the people with balance problems due to sudden loss of support.

8. FEAR OF NOISE (ACOUSTICOPHOBIA)

Starts with the fear of loud noises and escalates with loss of control and the impossibility of handling the situation.

Most of this fear is related to PTSD and is common to people who experienced war or got into an accident.

They become very sensitive to noise and end up in seclusion and isolation avoiding people and parties.

9. FEAR OF EATING

It is a phobia characterized by loss of appetite and the incapacity of swallowing liquid or solid food.

If those people are forced to eat, the only relief they are able to gain is by vomiting.

This phobia is connected to ANOREXIA NERVOSA, which is considered more like a psychological disorder.

It is followed by severe weight loss, dehydration, slowing of body growth process and menstrual cycle cessation in women.

Fear of eating can be also caused by a low self-esteem due to overweight condition or other rejection issues and is very harmful to the individual.

10. ARACHNOPHOBIA (FEAR OF SPIDERS)

It is called a "prepared fear" and is common in humans even though less than 1 percent of the spider species are harmful.

This phobia is triggered by the size, color and texture of the spider even though the science says that the smaller are ones that are more dangerous.

Many people develop OCD (OBSESSIVE COMPULSIVE DISORDERS)

In addition, out of fear of finding a spider hidden somewhere they will over wash their fruit and vegetable or check and fumigate the house excessively often.

This phobia is associated with feelings of disgust or fear of being touched by this creature; it is named a "crawling effect" (similar to the repulsion to snakes).

A very common therapy for children suffering from fear of spiders is group therapy based on poetry and singing.

I will stop here in the hope that this chapter was more interesting than boring and I will present a few of the treatments, therapies and procedures that help cope with most of the phobias fears anxiety and stress that debilitate the people.

Healing the fears

FACE YOUR FEAR AND DOUBTS AND A NEW
WORLD WILL OPEN TO YOU

ROBERT KIYOSAKI

We learn about different types of fears and phobias and now it is time to find out several approaches and treatments to get better.

It is not by suppressing the fears but learning to live with them, cope with them, face them, make peace with them and mostly understand them.

This is a very personal approach and depends on every individual point of view.

1. SLOW BREATHING

The most powerful accessible tool to calm your mind and body is slow breathing.

You activate your para sympathetic nervous system (rest and digest).

The signal sent to the brain is that you are not in danger and there is no need to hyperventilate.

Let the breath run slowly without forcing it and focus on it.

Breathe through your belly resting your hands on your stomach; inhale, hold your breath, exhale hold your breath.

When exhaling purse your lips and release the air like by blowing a candle.

Repeat it for 5 minutes and do the exercise every time you fell stressed or agitated.

2. POSITIVE THINKING

Wake up with a happy mind, turn on the music or listen to an inspirational broadcast.

Do some light exercises and on your way to work smile and enlighten your day with positive thinking.

Before you go to bed feed your body with messages of love and bliss.

No matter what the circumstances are, fell the power of achieving good things.

3. PMR (PROGRESSIVE MUSCLE RELAXATION)

It means tensing and relaxing your muscles in an exaggerated way.

Tense your fists, forehead, eyes, mouth, stomach and shoulders for 15 seconds and release.

With this exercise, the brain will recognize and rethink the state of the emotion.

4. REWARD YOURSELF

Short-term rewards will make the fear more inaccessible and the accomplishments more enjoyable.

It has actually the same structure as a reward payment.

Fantasize about cultural events, travel, spa days and make it happen.

Start by "earning points" and when you have enough just do it.

It will help you accomplish tasks easier when they feel difficult at the beginning.

It will increase your motivation through raising the dopamine level.

By shifting away your attention from panic, you rewire your brain into becoming more confident into achieving your goal.

It will also improve your **MYELINATION** process (strengthening the pathways between the neurons.)

5. HEALING THERAPY

Takes place with the assistance of a **HEALER** who places the hands on the individual and transports good energy to the patient's body.

The therapy might be very helpful by leading from a state of denial to a state of hope.

It connects better the body and mind reducing the stress symptoms.

6. HUMOR THERAPY

A created state of euphoria which is absolutely welcomed anytime.

Provides a sense of wellbeing, freedom and attracts the positive attention and energy.

By laughing we reduce the emotional pain and strengthen the defense mechanism of the body resulting in better coping with fears.

7. POETRY AND MUSIC

It is a way to see the beauty of the art instead of focusing on the brutal response of the body toward stress.

It is common in treating the children but also adults.

It increases relaxation by returning the contracted muscles to a state of relaxation, which has a positive impact on the body immunity.

8. PUPPET THERAPY

Mostly used for children.

It helps express ideas and states of mind that cannot be otherwise expressed and are considered unacceptable to talk about with a therapist.

It is designed to encourage the spontaneity and discourage aggression and conflicts.

9. WILL THERAPY

It is a form of psychotherapy and was first introduced in nineteen-forties in Austria.

It is the ability to self-express and find a way to separate yourself from the people and situations that trigger the state of stress.

It helps solving the conflict between dependence and independence.

10. CBT (COGNITIVE BEHAVIORAL THERAPY)

It is the process of learning strategies to move past your anxious thoughts and behaviors.

It treats anxiety and produces long lasting changes in the brain patterns.

11. ECT (ELECTROSHOCK THERAPY)

It is lately declined in the favor of medication, healing therapy, aromatherapy, activities and interpersonal contacts with other people.

12. PIT (PSYCHO-IMAGINATION THERAPY)

It is the use of stepping into an imaginary scenario helping the individual to wake up imagination and creativity.

It helps altering the ways of wrongfully fighting with anxieties.

13. TERRAP (TERRITORIAL APPREHENSIVE PROGRAM)

It is an approach to evaluate and diagnostic the patient before administering medication.

It is usually done in a 20 sessions program, individual or in a group and includes different stimuli.

The individual experiences a pleasant picture, a pleasant smell, soft rocking chair movements, nice relaxing sounds, tactile sensations like hugging.

All can be accompanied by field trips lectures or movies and are considered natural tranquilizers.

Patients develop realistic, logic and positive thinking.

14. SUBLIMINAL TECHNIQUES

It consists of visual stimuli that are flashed on a computer screen; the image is very fast processed and the individual is more or less unaware of what he sees in a flash.

The split image affects a level below consciousness and, depending on the message, it helps with various problems.

For instance one of the flashed image can be "I AM FEARLESS" and automatically the brain becomes calmer in the phobic moments.

15. YOGA

It is a method from the third century BC and means to find balance and achieve relaxation.

It increases energy, fights anxiety and helps the body to better functioning.

It consists of different postures and stretching exercises accompanied by OHM sounds, mantras and calming music.

It is based on the observation of the individual mental health and body condition.

It stimulates the CHAKRA centers of energy in the body and by this stimulates the spinal cord and the glands.

It creates a state of self-awareness and wellbeing and conserves the focus and energy.

There are some postures in Yoga that I want to mention:

1. ASANAS (physical postures)
2. PRANAYAMA (self-aware breathing)
3. SAMADTI (state of silence and bliss)

The sound of HUM means that the Universe is within us all the time.

In Yoga, we move from physical body to vital and mental body and further to the body of BLISS.

16. MEDITATION

It is a learned technique involving deep relaxation brought on by a sound of OHM and breathing exercises.

It is well known that the meditation decreases the heart rate and blood pressure and brings a state of peace.

It is a very ancient self-discipline introduced by the yogis and Tibetan monks and it is a simple and powerful thing.

During the meditation the alpha brain waves indicate a deep relaxation and people claim that they are less irritable, can develop more interpersonal relationships and regain the serenity of the mind and the balance of the body.

There are still a lot of misconceptions and some people consider this approach time consuming and find it hard to concentrate.

Only by practicing we see the benefit of the meditation and all the misconceptions disappear.

There is here one of the exercises based on visualization:

Sit comfortable in a chair with the back upright or of the floor in a very relaxed position.

Close your eyes and keep them closed through the whole visualization process.

Take a deep breath; inhale the pure loving energy of the Universe... exhale the fear and pain.

Once more...in and out.

Visualize a ball of light approaching the top of your head and slowly making its way through your body bringing bliss and serenity.

Start with relaxing the top of the head where we have the Crown Chakra and slowly go down and work your breath slowly through your face first.

Let the light travel through your body.

Relax the face, jaw and then focus on your neck, chest, solar plexus.

Continue with your shoulders, arms, fingers and down to the pelvis, legs and toes.

Activate all the Chakras with the healing light, breathe and release the tension.

Now ask yourself...

What if I had no fear?
What would I do next?
How does fear relate to me?
Do I enjoy the actual peace of mind?
Can I move on with confidence?

Feel the soothing light going through your body and then let it slip into the Earth taking with it the fear and pain.

See yourself empowered by the SOURCE and feel the confidence and love.

Stay in this state and breathe into the new feeling.

Slowly, when you are ready get present in your chair and open your eyes.

Enjoy the deliciousness of the actual state of bliss, stretch and smile.

Don't rush, have patience and faith.

IT IS ALL HERE AND YOU GOT IT.

Now you are at peace tuned to your Higher Self.

17. MINDFUL MEDITATION

It is part of the practice of meditation but more enhanced.

This Buddhist practice dates back over thirty five hundred years ago and it is based on nonjudgmental thinking and being in the present moment.

It helps rewire the brain to a more mindful state of mind by working on the "resilience muscles".

The benefit of this practice is reducing the size of the AMYGDALA and activating the CORTEX in order to create plans that are more beneficial.

The constant practice strengthens the bond between amygdala and cortex and reduces stress making room for empathy and compassion.

18. ZEN THERAPY

It is an anxiety reducing meditative technique.

The word ZEN means meditation in Chinese.

The movement started in China in the seventh century and later spread to Japan.

The process is called ZAZEN and it is practiced with open eyes, back upright and a firmly balanced position.

The state of concentration is called KOAN, and it consists of different questions meant to observe the flow of thoughts in a detached state.

The goal of the process is reaching SATORI, which is considered the ultimate goal in life without control.

19. DRUG THERAPY, but until we go there we should think twice... it always comes with side effects and addiction.

Most of the time our running emotional pain becomes a long life suffering.

With all those therapies we can avoid inevitable situations.

Be open minded accept the discomfort rather than fight and don't let the fear rule you in life.

Make mistakes and don't be afraid to go the opposite way just because the fear tells you.

Trust yourself and accept the help.

Encourage yourself by telling you:

I have survived difficult moments.
It will be OK soon.
I am strong.
Anxiety is not me.

TAKE ONE STEP AT A TIME!

Fear And Intuition

NEVER UNDERESTIMATE THE POWER OF YOUR
GUT FEELINGS.

ADRIANA CARA

Intuition is described as an emotional, unreasonable inexplicable feeling attributed mostly to women.

The logic and information deny intuition even if it is right.

Still some of the scientists rely on the powers of intuition knowingly or unknowingly because we are built to see only what we want to see.

Mostly we feel the intuition in our "guts" and we say to ourselves "I already knew it".

The root of the word is the Latin "TUERE" and means to guard or protect.

The intuition is learned and the signals are meaningful and important.

They differ according to urgency and we have to respect the ranking.

The most important intuitive signal with great urgency is FEAR.

The next level is DOUBT, SUSPICION, ANXIETY, WORRIES and all come with physical sensations.

Karl Menninger said, "When we consider the precise intuitive signals and evaluate them without denial you will be notified by a danger worth your attention".

When you receive a message and through intuition, you evaluate it, the fear will stop immediately.

Intuition is exactly the opposite of living in fear.

The signal that activates intuition is very sharp and comes as a tool of protecting your body from danger.

As we all know by now one of the rules of the fear is that you fear something that is not happening now.

What you think is just the link to the real fear.

In 1960 there was a study seeking to determine that a single word can have a great psychological impact.

The word SHARK means more fear than RAPE or INCEST.

The fact that a creature can show and attack without warning is beyond intuition and as a result we stay away from the ocean.

It creates panic mostly because in front of the shark we lose the sense of identity and we are just a piece of meat.

The loss of identity for humans is stronger that death itself.

We are not afraid of humans that are far more dangerous than sharks because the danger from humans is far more complicated.

Besides dangers like planes, cars, chemicals our biggest threat is the ANGRY HUMAN BEING.

The fear of humans is constantly there, you cannot avoid it, period.

Fear is necessary and valuable as a component of life while pain and worry are destructive.

Listen to your fear, use your intuition but if you don't have a reason to fear don't manufacture it.

Ernst Becker explains that man's fears are fashioned out of the ways in which he perceives the world even though the world seems to be a safe place.

We are here to survive and take risk in extraordinary moments every day.

With intuition and confidence activated, we can avoid great fears and recognize the survivals signs quicker and better.

Fear And Violence

THE MOST DIFFICULT MOMENT IN A WAR IS
SIGNING A TREATY OF PEACE.

ADRIANA CARA

Violence is in our culture and therefore easy to tolerate even if it is a destroying force.

It is part of our species, it is in our genes and the humans climb at the top of the violence hierarchy having only one important pray: OURSELVES.

The violence gene is called D4DR and it influences the behavior of many violent criminals or kids that will become later assassins or bank robbers.

The geneticist Irving Gottesman says: "Under a different scenario and different environment the same person will become a hero in Bosnia".

People would do anything to avoid pain and fear caused by violence.

This is the cause of the little understanding about the connection between feeling, thinking and behaving.

We become more terrified and the growing feeling becomes more painful.

Some run from anger to fear, some use abusive power, which translate as a lack of courage.

Most people show cruelty and violence to mask their own fears; it is ultimately a lack of self-worth.

The rate of violence in US is ten times greater than in any other Western civilized country with an alarming rate among women and children.

We hope that the future will show us a MAP OF PERSONALITY together with the height and weight of each and every individual, but until then we have to treat our children lovingly and humanly with the hope that the violence gene will not show the teeth.

Even if we live in modern times, we still have a Stone Age mind sometimes.

We are competitive and territorial.

The source of violence is in everyone but what changes is just our way to justify it.

Many people kill in case someone harm a loved one; it justifies in many ways the wars.

In the recent Ukrainian war soldiers kill each other, some because they love their country and fight for liberty, the others blindfolded by a despotic tyrant.

Soldiers, civilians and children are buried in mass graves...in the twenty first century, and the others are under the threat of the atomic bomb.

No matter how much help is on the way to support the Ukrainian soldiers, it will not alleviate the pains for the people who lose the loved ones in a bloody war or the immense loss of innocent people who die every day (100 Ukrainian soldier per day, if not more) adding unthinkable damage.

In the meantime, here in US we witness the horrors of the mass shooting.

Four brutal killings done by teenagers that have the right to buy guns and use them without license; kids are killed as well and teachers and the country is in mourning for the fourth time in three weeks.

Still there is big political debate, too political... about passing the bill banning the possessions of guns.

What is happening?

Did we lose our human values and the sense of compassion and peace as a nation?

Violent people are mostly in a state of denial, suffer from deep anxieties and consider themselves the victims.

They appear to be "nice" people who behave normally. It is a strategy to reach their goals and this is not a real characteristic of goodness.

Their smiley face implies obsession, death, mental illness, child abuse, spouse abuse or children who kill their parents.

One of the most common type of violence is VIOLENCE IN A COUPLE but many abused women choose to stay in this situation and not get out of it.

Like a battered child, a battered woman gets a feeling of powerful relief when the incident ends, and after it they see their partners like the ones who deliver peace and a better life.

The beaten ones become dull to violence and fear.

Between incidents the violent ones becomes gentle, loving, calm, and supportive and victims seem to enjoy those pleasant breaks.

The Domestic Council shows that every woman in need has a bed in the shelter but they refuse to go there for help.

There is also the alternative of RESTRAIN ORDER which is an optional way to stop violence, but most of the time after 6 months of restrictions the couple reunites and the cycle of violence begins again with even more violence.

Unfortunately, the Government cannot act when emotional situations are involved because freedom is an option not a law and people act accordingly.

Another type of violence triggers CHILDREN.

After much research it is confirmed that many child molesters have been abused as children or treated with neglect and humiliation.

Violence is present at WORK place where people interact a lot and fight for better title and better money.

Again, with all the warnings, the threats and violent acts are ignored.

GUN VIOLENCE is a very sensitive subject.

For some the banning of guns is equivalent to a government impose castration.

The real problem is not the gun control but the BULLET CONTROL.

The guns technology should require more safety features.

In the meantime, if you have a gun, instead of looking for safety triggers you should lock the gun in a safe place, away from family and kids.

A company called Sesame sells locks for the guns with a special personal combination.

In a nutshell, the majority of violent people started like any of us but the difference consists of the lesson they learned.

We tend to believe that the violence is a mystery beyond understanding and cannot be explored or avoided.

This is a myth and the victims suffer while the criminals prosper.

The prediction of violence is not as difficult as winning a lottery ticket.

Out there are people who show signs of violence that have to be interpreted.

All those red signals together with intuition and fears will protect our loved ones and us.

VIOLENCE TOWARD ANIMALS

I consider this type of violence even crueler than human violence.

The animals have no voice to talk about their fears or pains and they blindly love and trust the humans.

I am an animal lover and it breaks my heart to see and talk about animal violence.

Animals should be killed and given thanks after they die only when they save people from hunger (Native American culture).

Animals represent loyalty, freedom, hope, kindness.

In India, as we all know, the cows are sacred and they roam the streets without any threats.

Same with mice that are fed in the churches (I personally don't agree with this custom because of health reason, but it is a very personal opinion).

We misinterpret their aggression when we invade their territory or harm the species (tigers, sharks).

"Men were the only animals that slaughtered their own kind by millions, and turned the landscape into a waste of shells, craters and barbed wire.

Perhaps the human race would wipe itself out completely and leave the world to the birds and trees."

Perhaps that would be for the best". (Kenn Follett)

I will dedicate my next chapter to our beloved animals, our furry unconditional loving friends.

Fear And Fur

WE CAN JUDGE THE HEART OF A MAN BY HIS TREATMENTS OF ANIMALS

IMMANUEL KANT

I feel a lot of love and joy writing about our closest furry friends and how important and significant they are in our life.

They give us unconditional love, heal our pain and fears in tormented moments and look in our eyes showing how much they love us without words.

I am an animal lover.

I love every creature that moves and I am in constant awe about the beauty and the diversity of the animal kingdom.

Every time I go horseback riding I make a soul connection with the horse first by whispering words of love in his ear.

My love for turtles made me travel to Galapagos to see them in their habitat.

As a child I used to have a family of frogs that I adored, each and every one with a distinct name.

Because I want to dedicate this chapter specifically to our beloved cats and dogs I want to emphasize their importance in our life and the presence in the history and folklore and also as their role as healers in our life and in the medical field.

CATS have super senses of smell, much more developed than human senses.

They can see in an ultraviolet field, they can feel a phone call before it rings. They can sense someone's death before it comes.

People claim that cats can sense the presence of the ghosts and chase them away just with a hiss.

In Egypt the cats were sacred and killing a cat was punished with death.

They were considered magical and we see the presence of a cat-headed goddess called Bast in the old mythology manuscripts.

Cats accompanied high rank figures in the afterlife journey as we can find their remains in sacred Egyptian tombs.

Hemingway was in love with polydactyl cats (extra toes) and we still see some of these cats in his Florida Key old residence.

For some people in England some cats bring good luck, some steal souls.

DOGS are physically more attached to humans and they serve as companions for the elderly, blind or sick people or take part in the healing process in hospitals or nursing homes.

They respond to commands when their name is called and feel the affection stronger and quicker than cats.

They can feel if a person has a tendency to suicide. They have different responses to the smell of FEAR or HAPPINESS.

They are present in the treatment of severe case of Alzheimer and dementia by helping reduce anxiety, irritability, depression and loneliness.

They smell and feel changes in blood pressure in patients or even more, they detect cancer.

They offer something that people cannot offer the same way: interaction, companionship, love and fun.

They feel when you are sad or hurt, they are not critical or judgmental.

They are the ones to find people lost in winter snow avalanches.

They are adopted by homeless people and help each other in moments of fear.

There are also programs in the penitentiaries where the inmates have to care for a dog as part of improving the state of anger and violence of the incarcerated.

No need to say how helpful dogs are in wars and in detecting drugs or victims after an earthquake.

Dogs "smell "death and are used to locate the cadavers.

Dogs don't leave the grave of the beloved deceased master and grieve for long time and can wait years for a person who left or disappeared.

The bond between the pet and the owner is so strong that it can happen at the level of thoughts.

The British researcher Rupert Sheldrake sustains that cats and dogs can reach their owner's mind.

His studies and experiments reinforce this theory.

It is known that dogs get very excited for a walk especially when their masters hold the leash and go to the door.

Sheldrake places the experimental dog outside their homes away from the owner.

He asks the individual to mentally access the thought of taking the dog outside without any physical connection with the dog at random hours.

The dog starts to wiggle his tails and starts circling around the door in anticipation to the event of going out with the owner.

This event is startling and it proves the telepathic connection between owner and pet.

CATS AND DOGS are our friends and healers.

Let's love and respect them.

I will write a few emotional stories about our furry friends.

MY STORY

I used to have three cats, all adorable, stray independent cats.

They use to come and go out of my house as they pleased.

My favorite was Baby, a tigress kitten, an absolute beautiful cat that was highly courted by the males cats from the neighborhood.

Of course, the inevitable happen and she got pregnant so I took her to the doctor.

She became so fond of me she used to stay in front of the computer and touch the screen playing with the images.

The nights she roamed the neighborhood but in the morning was knocking at the door with her paw to let her in.

When I had a pain, she knew where to sit and release the discomfort.

The other two were older and more distant.

A sad event drove me to send two of them to a shelter because one of them was poisoned and died in my arms...what a painful day!

I also used to be a babysitter for my friend's dogs and spend memorable moments with my dearest dogs most of the time on the floor covered in kisses and love.

CARMEN'S STORY

I have to mention that my friend sent me such a beautiful essay about her cat that I had to copy it in my chapter the very way it was written.

It stirred a lot of tears...

"I received Topi (Topaz) from the daughter of my son's former teacher.

He was a Birman breed three or four months old with eyes the color of the beautiful summer sky.

From the moment I saw him I knew that he would be my most loyal soul mate.

We didn't need any words because we understood each other just by looking at one another.

When I was coming back from work he was waiting patiently glued to the door.

First thing I checked his little plate to see if he had enough water or milk.

Sometimes I gave him the last drop of milk instead of putting it in my coffee.

Oh… his brown fur and tail…

Sometimes he made a sound like a little bird chirp, soft and soothing.

He was mostly vegetarian, absolutely crazy about melon, beans, and cabbage.

After neutering I put him in a basket overnight with the night light on to watch him.

I was dozing while he slowly moved, he wanted to go to the bathroom...he had a common sense, a real gentle cat.

My Topi was my healer, my medication, my real soul mate.

After 20 years and 7 months, he went to Heaven but his mortal body is buried under my balcony where yellow flowers grow.

He was with me in moments of desperation, anguish and fear unlike any human being.

He lived the longest possible just to be with me and not leave me alone…

I will miss him forever!

ULRIKA'S STORY

Shortly after her beloved Rottweiler Pinky died, Ulrika had a dream.

The dog was trying to wake her up and send her to lock the doors and windows of the house.

The morning of the next day police was ringing the doorbell; there was a case of burglary and assault next door the previous night.

She ended her story by telling me that Pinky's soul saved her life.

It sounds unreal, right?

WHY DO WE LOVE OUR PETS?

A new study published in the "Journal of science" reveals why we feel so close to our furry friends.

There is a hormone called oxytocin that floods new moms when they are attached to their babies.

The same hormone is released in both humans and dogs when they interact, cuddle or even look into each other's eyes.

A dog loves his owner five times more than a cat, but it doesn't mean that cats should be neglected.

Over the process of domestication, dogs prefer the companionship of the humans to the companionship of other dogs.

Dogs love human kisses and respond quickly and positively because they know that this is an act of love and tenderness.

They tend to bond with the people who give them the most attention.

There are many ways to show your dog that you love him:

Rub his ears.

Lean on him.

Gaze into his eyes.

Snuggle and kiss him.

If the dog licks you it means he looks for affection or just act on their wild instincts.

Dogs fall in love much more easily than people do. They adapt to protect us.

They have similar genes to humans; these genes are linked to human sweetness.

And if you think that you don't love your pet enough...there is always a solution: LOVE THEM MORE!

"We don't know what happen with dogs when they pass.

They take a peace of our soul with them while they leave." (T.J. Klune)

The Gift Of Fear

TO ESCAPE FEAR YOU HAVE TO GO THROUGH
IT, NOT AROUND.

RICHIE NORTHON

It takes courage to face your fear and if you think that fear is a problem there is always a way to solve it; the bigger the problem the more you will get out of solving it.

Courage is the willingness to feel your fear in a scary world.

Taking a much harder and more painful road makes us complete human beings.

Willfully going through darkness to become known is the right way.

You have the courage to play the game that our ancestors never tried and shift the patterns of fear for you and the people you know or meet.

Trusting yourself and being curios about the FEAR is a big thing but making friends with the fear and honor it is different.

Being on the side of your fears will give your insight, motivation, clear vision and the gates of the Wisdom will open for you.

We cannot heal the relationship with ANGER, SHAME, and MISERY until we heal the relationship with FEAR and reach a higher level of consciousness.

You don't have to go back in time and get lost in the process of remembering and healing certain moments in your life; you just have to start a relationship with your fear right now.

You don't have to plan a specific time to make friends with fear or conquer it...fear is too smart for it.

Don't make a goal of it because it will create tension and the expectations might be bigger than the outcome.

Stop hoping into a fearless future because this will lead to more unanswered questions.

Take Buddha's example... he reached the moment of Enlightenment in a moment looking at Venus; he didn't ask, he just reached it.

Stop any form of resistance and open yourself to the unexplained events in life, the "not knowing-not thinking-not seeing "moments.

LET IT BE AND JUST BE IT!

If you hear the voice of fear just listen to it, feel it and humor it!

Reprogram your brain with a new way of thinking, like programming a new computer.

If you try therapy, yoga or other procedures to suppress the fear and you feel that you have enough of it just walk out of the session, look fear in the eyes and give a bow.

You can do infinite work while the therapy is limited; start to feel in order to heal.

Once you challenge and overcome fear you will enjoy it...you are smarter than fear.

Pay attention to your feelings, be yourself, feel the emotions, let the body speak for itself and connect with the bigger YOU.

This is who you really are.

The easy way is to surrender.

Not knowing and not fighting is where the Wisdom lies.

Listen to the inner voice that whispers, "I am the fear".

Speak from your heart, put a hand on your heart and feel the voice.

Speak from your head, put your hand on your head and feel the voice.

Ask yourself: "Am I afraid?"

Notice how you feel and answer with the truth, your truth.

It might hurt...you might want to resist...

Create a practice out of it, a satisfying routine to do it when you feel the darkness of the fear approaching.

See where the truth lies, create a relationship with your fear and observe its patterns.

Who is in charge with your fear?

Whose job is it to be afraid?

Is it you?

Always go back to the state of "let it be".

Trust your body.

If you are not ready to face the fear tell yourself that today is not a good day for it.

You will get there, you will own your fear, you will have clarity and liberation and you will feel empowered.

Get into a state of wonder; get ready for the fear to come back each time on its terms.

Don't do anything.

Just experience this beautiful ride, feel the energy of the moment and emerge with it.

In ZEN, there is a cool saying:

"Kiss the dragon, it becomes a maiden,
Kiss the tiger, it becomes the Buddha,
Kiss the demon, it becomes love".

The demon of love can turn into love through love.

Have your own experience.

The benefits of honoring the fear are not just shrinking your problems but expanding the best parts of your life.

You become full of wisdom like a magician or shaman wise with fear.

Just thinking how important fear is in the process of evolution of the human race gives it a lot of credit; that alone deserves a bow of respect.

Many people do great things not by disputing fear but because of the motivation that it creates.

Fear is here to help you change into a better version of yourself.

It will make you move forward, evolve and not stagnate, break free and grow into what you become next.

Even LOVE is more interesting when we are afraid and vulnerable; it makes our heart beat faster and stronger.

What you feel for yourself you will feel for the others and if you honor the discomfort of fear you will be more compassionate with the others; it will bring more peace and friendship around you.

Imagine a world at peace with fear, full of courage, love and confidence.

You will breathe fresh air, expand and go everywhere you want.

You will find balance, happiness, satisfaction and reach any goal.

Hold on to your fear, IT IS A GIFT FROM UNIVERSE!

The more you feel the fear the stronger you become.

When you are afraid feel the fear, when you are restless just be restless, when you are at peace just feel the peace; it is spiritual intelligence.

Own your discomfort, seek and explore your life with wisdom; this will be a journey of a lifetime.

All your feelings starting with fear are absolutely necessary for your success in life and they will shape the person that you really are.

Once we make a shift in feeling our fear the world will be a different place.

Fear is the story of your life, it is evolution and it is up to you if you honor it or not.

Fear will stay with us no matter what. If you want to be a better person or do your daily prayers, it is not a punishment that we have to accept in order to overcome obstacles.

It is the light that guides us, the strength and the ability to split open your heart and show the world who you really are.

We long for acceptance, understanding, freedom.

When the fear replaces the feelings of safety then it is time to ask ourselves:

Where does the fear begin?
Am I afraid?
Why am I afraid?
So what if I am afraid?

It is OK to feel afraid as long as you are open to explore your fears.

We are born free but our culture and religion tells us to be afraid.

As vulnerable persons we are told to change in order to be accepted, loved, cherished or seen.

As we grow older the fear grows with us and divide into hundreds of other fears until it becomes impossible to remember how it all began and why we continue to blame ourselves.

Most of the time we carry other people's fears; parents involuntary and unknowingly transmit the fears to their children believing that this is a way to safety to follow the same path in life like the one they did.

In a way, it is a sort of protection but it stops us from evolving and experiencing things that can fulfill and shape us in the person we want to be.

The most complicated fear is the fear of who we are; it is difficult to change our body, to make someone love us or to change the surroundings.

But everyone has fears and it is very important to take a decision before a reasonable concern becomes an irrational beast.

And we all have our brain to protect us.

I let my fear scare me many years of my life because I really didn't know that FEAR can become my closest friend; it knows who I really am and who I want to be, where I want to go and what I want to do.

Once I accepted it and I stepped back and recognized the reality of fear I felt free.

Instead of being afraid of walking a different path I started with small steps slowly with the fear by my side.

And then I could uncover many hidden truths and big wishes...

I just started to look FEAR in the eyes...

An experiment by the Italian psychologist Giovanni Caputo asks people to look in the mirror for ten minutes, concentrating on their faces.

Some see a distorted version of their faces or even a different face looking back at them, so by the end of the session many fail to recognize the person in the mirror as themselves.

There are so many hidden inside of us and we pretend that fear doesn't exist but as in Caputo's experiment fear appears in the most startling ways.

When I look in the mirror, I see the childlike vulnerability looking back at me, the small person that sometimes is unloved and forgotten.

When I close my eyes, I feel a void of different colors moving behind my eyes connecting with my dreams, my wishes and my hopes...

Next time you feel fear rattling inside your body draw it closer and hug yourself.

By recognizing the fear and the changes they bring to your body and your brain you can alleviate the symptoms and discomfort that comes with it.

Fear will speak to you in different tongues: that can be a monologue, your parents voicing their fears or your inner voice telling you that you are not good enough.

Just like you start a conversation with a friend do the same with your fear and listen carefully at what it has to say.

Venture into the world of Unknown side by side with your fear because in the mystery of it you will find the most beautiful places to visit.

We visit the great Unknown many times in our lives but every time we discover a beautiful detail, a pleasant surprise but also a danger or a disappointment.

Just open your eyes and heart to the GIFT OF FEAR the way you do with a beautiful view of a sunrise.

Experience the freedom of this feeling and if you are not ready today there will be a tomorrow or another day.

There will be a magic in every new beginning and the fear will be with you and help you find the beauty in your vulnerability.

Actress Charlotte Rampling says:

"If you want to give anything worthwhile of yourself you have to be completely exposed."

The most beautiful people are the one bearing the scars of loss, disappointment, heartbreak, struggle and pain.

We are all the same and even if we are so far apart we are looking at the same stars.

The Map Of Our Heart

AS HUMAN BEINGS WE CAN ONLY EXPERIENCE LIFE EMOTIONALLY.

EDUARDO BERICAT
(SOCIOLOGY PROFESSOR)

Humans means connection with ourselves and connection with the others by establishing a common ground, by understanding and expressing our feelings and emotions.

We learn to label our feelings and with the help of a vocabulary we can give nuances to our emotions; that can really be a transformation.

Every solid ground has an anchor and we have this in ourselves; it will help us to communicate emotions and human experiences with the others or with ourselves.

Most of the time we believe that our emotions and feelings come from the heart even though they are all processed by the brain.

Imagine your heart as a big map and the emotions like big or small cities each connected by roads, rivers or bridges.

We have no idea where we are on the map or where we are going but we see that we can find our way if we see the connections.

We just need a right map and the truest self to explore it.

"With an adventurous heart and the right map we can travel anywhere and never fear losing ourselves" (Brene Brown)

Acknowledgment

THE MOST IMPORTANT KIND OF FREEDOM IS
TO BE WHO YOU REALLY ARE

JIM MORRISON

This book that you are reading, my friend, is a book about fear, loneliness, longing and hiding, about being frightened, about what we can find outside of our shell.

It is about the hope of being loved and recognized and about the hidden fervent desire of a life full of love and nurturing.

This is a book about you and me, about the window between us that waits to be opened.

This is a book written in moments of pain and despair, sickness and tears and it will haunt me for the rest of my life.

IT IS A BOOK ABOUT HEALING.

It is a book that wants to be held.

It is a book filled with raw emotions, honesty and grace.

I hope from the bottom of my heart that it will be useful.

I will recognize with humility the greatest inspiration given by wonderful books and skillful writers:

1. Deepak Chopra
   The future of God
   Life after death
2. Kristen Ulmer
   The art of fear
3. Gavin de Becker
   The gift of fear
4. Susan Jeffers
   Feel the fear
5. Debra Kissen
   Rewire your anxious brain
6. Ronald M. doctor PHD
   The A to Z phobias, fears and anxieties
7. Brene Brown
   The atlas of the heart
8. Sadguru
   Death, an inside story
9. Meera Lee Pate
   My friend fear
10. 10. Jamie Moore
    Friendship with God
11. Charles H. Spurgeon
    Power of prayer
12. Neale Donald Walsch
    Conversation with God
13. Ruth Graham
    Fear not tomorrow, God is already there
14. Raymond Moody MD.
    Life after life
15. T.J Klune
    Under the whispering door
16. Elisabeth Kubler Ross MD.
    On life after death
17. Elisabeth Kubler Ross. MD
    On death and dying

18. Kenn Follett
    Fall of the giants
19. Tom Vitale
    In the weeds around the world and behind the scenes with Anthony Bourdain

I am humble and thankful to all my readers of my first book, **The art of love connection and marriage.**

You gave me wings and showed me that the impossible is possible.

Deep thanks to my dearest friend Carmen who took precious time in reading my manuscript and telling me the incredible story of love for her furry friend.

Thanks to my friend Audrey who gave me the precious idea of writing the chapter Fear and Fur; I hope that will bring a note of love and care to my book.

Thank you Zoila for helping me choose the right cover, the right symbol and the right color showing the fear in the color spectrum.

Than you to my dearest Bo who listened to my ideas, fears and contradictions that came with this project.

She is my fearless critic.

Stephen Weirich, my wonderful doctor thank you.

He gave me hope in the moments of pain and sickness and motivated me to write this book.

My first book lays on his night table...

And finally THANK YOU my dearest friend and reader who took the time to read my humble thoughts.

Thanks to you I can do what I love the most: WRITING!!!

Heart is a sea,
Language is shore.
Whatever sea includes,
Will hit the shore.

RUMI

Printed in the United States
by Baker & Taylor Publisher Services